Dunge Bottom

Tales Of An Unconventional Aviator

To Park Hall Microlight Club,

This was how it was honest!!

First Published in 2011

John oct 2011

Published by Crooked Hat Publishing Ltd
Copyright © John Clarke 2011
Printed By Lightning Source Ltd
John Clarke has asserted his right to be identified as the author
of this work in accordance with the Copyright, Designs and
Patent Act 1988
Cover Photograph Richard Sheppard
Crooked Hat Publishing
An imprint of
Paperweight Press
Reg. No. 07472140
www.crookedhatpublishing.com
A CIP catalogue record for this book is currently pending.
All photography © John Clarke/Richard Sheppard/Eric
Barfoot/Steve Thompson
ISBN 978-0-9568447-0-5

Dunge Bottom

Tales Of An Unconventional Aviator

John Clarke

There is one person amongst many of the early hang gliding and microlighting pioneers who I feel has never quite had the acclaim that they rightly deserved.

He was, and still is, not one of the flamboyant extroverts that bespeckle my flying world. Rather he is a quiet, honest, straight as they come, gentleman who has integrity and good old fashioned standards.

I started my flying on one of his early designs and worked my way through the huge range of hang gliders and microlights that he designed and built over many years.

I and so many others owe a huge debt to his enthusiasm and flair in bringing innovation to the sport that we all shared and loved. Some of my greatest flights and adventures were whilst flying his designs.

I therefore dedicate this book to Len Gabriels, the man behind Skyhook Hang Gliders, Oldham.

Foreword

The word 'Extreme' is a bit overused these days. We have extreme drinks, extreme holidays and, of course, extreme sports. All around us there is a plethora of advertising encouraging us to live life to the max, go for it and other tiresome phrases. As an older, although by no means old, member of the population this irritates me immensely, not because I wish I were living an extreme life, but because I did and frankly people these days would not know extreme if it slapped them in the face; which it couldn't because that sort of thing isn't allowed now either.

These days extreme means doing something out of the ordinary but as safely as is possible. Let me be clear, this is a good thing, no one should suffer as a result of their sport and every effort to make it safer should be welcomed...but. The lithe young extreme sportsmen and women of today have their padded fashions and Kevlar suits of armour. They are heroes to a new generation who buy their computer games and follow their styles living vicariously the life of their icons. When I see this I make a little noise, it's the noise you make when you try a blow an imaginary trumpet and rattle your lips together vigorously, sort of 'pthrrrrgh'.

It sounds derisory, because it is. You see my sports were hang gliding and microlighting and my time was the early seventies. Back then we did not wear Kevlar, we wore cardigans and safe flying was putting your cigarette out before you launched. It was not that we didn't want to be safe, we just didn't know how to do it...

To illustrate this, allow me to give you a statistic. The Health and Safety Executive states that the risk of death while hang gliding is currently one in sixteen thousand. This is safer than childbirth and much, much safer than driving and is a tribute to the work of the various bodies that have made the sport what it is. Compare this to my time. In the seventies one in every thousand flights was fatal. This was not so much 'extreme' as 'bloody dangerous'.

This is the story of me and my sport when I was a naïve young man looking for a little adventure. In flying I found it. People would try to build a flying machine, leap off a hill and learn on the way down. The level of ignorance was breathtaking and the attrition rate was unsustainable. Although many 'how to' books have been written about these subjects, this book is definitely a 'how not to'. It is a collection of tales about my experiences, some of the characters I met and how the sport changed my life. The events actually happened and the people and places did, and do, exist. There has been no embellishment.

The people in this book do not have their names on sports drinks and they did not make millions from endorsements but their success and failures helped shape the sport we know today. So, with this in mind, I encourage you to sally forth and enjoy what has been written knowing that these times and events will never be allowed to happen again.

1

Norman and The Cloud

I was lying in the bracken at the top of Congleton Cloud, near Congleton, soaking up the sun and watching the spoonbills circling high under the fluffy white cumulus clouds which dotted the bright blue sky. In the distance the huge dish of the Jodrell Bank radio telescope was glinting blindingly in the early spring sunshine. The Cloud is an eight hundred foot high escarpment covered with trees on the side that faced over the vastness of the Cheshire Plain and is a great hang gliding site in North Westerly winds. You had to park your car at the back of the hill and then walk about half a mile to the take off point along a meandering rock strewn path bordered by deep gorse and bracken.

I had already rigged my glider and was waiting for the wind to strengthen a bit before taking off. Relaxing in the undergrowth, I thought I heard the mischievous buzzing of yet another Horsefly. My thoughts returned to a similar time

Dunge Bottom

last year when, having been bitten by such a beast, I had developed a touch of mange. My reverie was interrupted by a commotion somewhere behind me. The commotion became louder until I could make out intermittent swearing and gasping as someone obviously struggled for breath whilst doing battle with the undergrowth. I stood up and my eyes fell upon Norman, a rotund man, pouring with sweat, red faced and with a pronounced limp, wearing spectacles with lenses like bottle bottoms. He carried a hang glider precariously balanced on his shoulder.

"Hi," I called out, "Hell of a walk isn't it?"

"Bloody right" he gasped "You'll not get me up here again,"

I left him to recover his strength and breath. Eventually he rigged his hang glider and was considering taking off. He limped over towards me to ask a few questions about flying here, as it was his first time at this site.

"So where is the best take off spot?" he asked. I duly pointed it out.

"And the landing field?"

"It's over there Norman, the long rectangular field with a farm track running across this end of it that leads to the big farm on the left, which is where you pay your site fees. Oh and be careful of the power lines that run along the side of the track, other than that it's a great landing field."

I couldn't help but notice that Norman seemed to take an inordinate amount of time peering myopically out towards the landing area, before he limped back towards his glider and readied for takeoff. I watched with interest, as Norman started to run blindly towards the edge of the cliff with an increasingly ridiculous gait. As he neared the edge I was horrified to see that his right leg fell completely off, landing in the thick bracken and leaving the empty leg of his flying suit flapping in the breeze.

"Bloody hell" was my spontaneous outburst as Norman continued to hop the last couple of paces towards the cliff edge before falling off and disappearing from view. Fearing the worst I ran towards the edge as fast as I could only to see him now flying out towards the bottom landing field.

"How the hell is he going to survive? I mean the blood loss must be enormous; surely he'll be dead by the time he gets there." I thought.

I watched Norman's imminent approach to the landing field with mounting horror. He seemed to be much lower than normal, although from the distance I was viewing I could have been wrong. No, I wasn't wrong at all, for there was an enormous blue flash as Norman flew into the eleven thousand volt power lines running along the track on the approach to the field.

"Bloody hell" I repeated, at a loss for more expansive repartee.

I expected him to fall to the ground but no; he and his glider just hung there like a huge bat. I couldn't decide, at that moment, whether to run down to hill to affect a rescue or just amble down. After all, he had lost a leg and been electrocuted so I suspected his chances of survival were quite small. There was a further complication of what to do with his leg. Should I just leave it for the crows and buzzards to feast on, should I take it down so that the body bag could include a complete human being? Albeit in pieces.

I gingerly went over to where the leg had fallen and started to root around in the knee high vegetation. I admit I feared what I might find as I am not the keenest where any form of blood or gore is concerned.

"Ah that explains it." I muttered out loud with some great relief. I had found his leg complete with Velcro and leather straps hanging from the top end of it.

"A false one, thank goodness for that"

I chose to nip back to my car with the leg, which I noted was actually quite heavy, and take a leisurely drive down to the field. About ten minutes later I fearfully drove down the farm track, dreading the scene that would greet me. Getting as near as I dare to Norman the bat, still dangling from the power cables, I stopped the car and slowly got out and walked haltingly towards the scene. As I approached I couldn't help but notice that there was a low droning sound coming from the hunched figure swinging gently from the wires and that smoke was slowly spirally up from Norman's flying gloves. I slowed my pace further and on finally arriving below Norman, I was greeted by a low continual...

"Bastard, Bastard, Bastard" emanating from Norman.

"Bloody hell, Norman, are you still alive?" I yelled up at him.

My fear and trepidation started to turn to anger.

"Anyway, what the hell are you on about?" I further enquired.

"Look at them, just look at them, sodding ruined, first time I've worn them" he spat out with venom.

"What the hell are you on about?" I felt the need to enquire again.

"My sodding gloves, brand new, first time I've worn them and now ruined" he said by way of an explanation.

At this point we both looked at what no doubt was originally a very smart pair of leather flying gloves which had now turned into a charred smoking mess due to the electricity which had recently coursed through them.

"And I've lost my leg again, how the bloody hell am I going to get that one back?" he continued, chuntering on as I departed the scene due to the arrival of the Fire Service.

John Clarke

Later talking to the University Hang Gliding Club that Norman belonged to, they confirmed their fears about Norman's safety. They didn't seem to have a problem with the leg, oh no, that was fine. It was just that he was registered blind as well.

That explains it then.

I couldn't help but wonder as I started the long drive back home as to how twisty and turny my life had become, when I could consider the previous event as something not particularly strange, in fact, almost run of the mill for me in my world. Perhaps, if you could indulge me, I should explain how I came to this point in my adventures.

The Beginning

Is this what my future holds, I mused, one May afternoon? I had just got married at an embarrassingly early age and found myself on honeymoon with my lifelong partner on a warmish Sunday afternoon, about seventy degrees Fahrenheit as I recall, (I am unsure as to whether Centigrade had yet been invented). A gentle onshore breeze ruffled the blue rinses of some of the assembled ladies both audience and competitors. Can you believe it? We were watching a crown green bowling match featuring the over seventies of the Hunstanton and Wells Next The Sea, Senior Ladies bowling teams at... Cromer, on our honeymoon, for pity's sake.

Surely there is more excitement to life than this?

Well as it turned out there wasn't, a short time later and quite unexpectedly I might add, the person I thought was going to be my lifelong partner disappeared with a part time wrestler.

Coincidentally I was also becoming bored my chosen career of quantity surveying. You might be interested to know that the actual official definition of a quantity surveyor in the building world is a professional thief. By that I mean

Dunge Bottom

that one is expected to under measure and therefore under pay sub contractors, whilst over measuring and therefore being over paid by the client. I also became obsessed with counting. At one time I learned, because I had to physically measure them, how many bricks there were in the Guardian Office Block in Lichfield and the exact details of the foul and storm drainage system at the new Burton and District Hospital.

As an aside, when I was a cub of a quantity surveyor working for Thomas Lowe & Sons Ltd., of Burton on Trent on a project at Willington Power Station, we had a site agent called Bernard. I mention Bernard as he injected a ray of sunshine and laughter into my now depressed world. You see, Bernard's teeth became a legend in our closed world of builders. I am trying my best to think of how to describe him adequately for you dear reader, let's try this...

He was in his fifties, lean bodied, about five foot eight tall with a very deeply lined face.

No, that's not good enough.

Have you heard of the central African tribe, the Katangans? They were, and probably still are, famous for decapitating their enemies and pickling the heads. This had the effect of both shrinking the head and causing unbelievably wrinkled skin, which had the colour and texture of very old leather! Well Bernard had this sort of face but his teeth were huge like tombstones and incandescently white. So white you needed sunglasses to view them. Unfortunately, this wasn't the end for our fascination, because not only were they painfully white but had a mind of their own in so much as they moved about seemingly at random whilst squeaking loudly. Builders and sub contractors would come from miles around to discuss phantom problems with the project just to experience

John Clarke

Bernard's teeth.

Actually, if you can bear with me for a further moment, am I the only one to notice old people, particularly men? You must know what I mean, they have been growing a blackhead on their nose or perhaps forehead for several decades. It is impossible not to stare fixedly at this whilst imagining squeezing it. One can imagine the crater left would be the size of Tycho, albeit not white nor on the moon. I know that one day I will not be able to resist having a go. I can also imagine the headlines in the local paper...

"Twenty year old male attacks pensioner over irresistible facial feature...........given fifty hours community service........."

Ah, great times.

Shortly after being left for the wrestler, and just before my twenty first birthday, my life changed in one morning. As usual I visited the bathroom, completed the normal bodily functions after which I cleaned my teeth. All very normal and boring I know, except when spitting out the toothpaste I was surprised to see that I completely missed the sink. "Odd" I thought. "Better have another go". Same result. "Becoming odder". I looked up at the mirror and recoiled in horror at the apparition before me. The left side of my face was completely paralysed and drooped to such an extent I couldn't close my mouth properly, and I couldn't close my left eye either.

"Shit!"

I called out to my family but the words, which I now pronounced "worms", didn't work. I couldn't even speak properly. Whistling was right out!

I immediately visited my GP (yes, you could get appointments very easily in those days) in a heightened state of tension. I was reassured to learn from him that it was caused by inflammation of a nerve that enters the skull just behind the ear, causing facial paralysis. "Phew" I thought. Now I know what I'm dealing with. "What's the prognosis?" I cheerfully asked, only to be told that there was no treatment and that it either gets better of its own accord or not at all. Not quite the answer I was hoping for. On further questioning, the GP was persuaded to tell me that most people don't recover from it.

"Bugger".

I have to be honest here and say that counting bricks and measuring drains could only sustain my interest for a little while, so eventually I dallied with other areas of the building industry with the inevitable result of being made redundant a couple of times. As you might imagine, I was feeling a little low, what with a failed marriage, paralyzed face and a boring job, life at twenty one was looking a little bleak. I needed to do something positive and not accept my current lot. With my palsy it was unlikely that I would win many favours with ladies unless I moved in darkness or took to wearing a bag. However, even if I did get close enough using said cover, or a bag, to get to the smooching stage, the continual drooling from the left side of my mouth would, I suspect, be ever so slightly abhorrent, not to mention messy. So I must ignore the normal aspirations and desires of a young twenty one year old male and concentrate on diversionary activities. I needed to grasp the situation by the throat and take control. In short, I needed excitement.

"Time to move on to pastures new", thought I, but what?

2

What Airfield?

On one bitterly cold November week end I went to Halfpenny Green aerodrome near Wolverhampton with Bradford, my best mate (although we weren't actually on first name terms at that point), as I had decided to enrol us both on a two day parachuting course. I had always imagined that airfields would have an air of excitement and romance, a tangible feeling of imminent adventure! I felt my alter ego to be Clarke of Adventure. One could almost imagine saying to the love of my life ...

"Just orf to the airfield m'dear"

Sounds exciting doesn't it? But no. The reality, as I was about to discover, was that they are cold windy and invariably wet, airfields, that is, not life partners. My romantic notions were decidedly dampened during my three month relationship with this particular site.

Dunge Bottom

This was my first visit to a small provincial airfield and I wasn't exactly sure what to expect. Runways, naturally, stretching off into the distance, a control tower, with those eerily blacked out windows that you see in the movies, perhaps a few empty deckchairs recently vacated by young men clad in their sheep skin flying coats with silk scarves fluttering out in the breeze as they rushed from the dispersal hut to the urgent sound of a klaxon. I could see them running wildly towards their waiting fighter aircraft, watched unemotionally by the compulsory black Labrador. I do believe that I may have read too much Biggles when younger and overdosed on my favourite film "Battle of Britain". On that cold autumn morning I looked across the expanse of the airfield and could sense a general air of neglect and sewage. Apparently there was a nearby sewage farm immediately up wind of us and that morning we were lucky enough to enjoy the aromas.

There were two large buildings, with enormous arched roofs. These were the hangers where we were to do our ground training and where the aircraft are kept. They seemed very flimsy and careworn being made out of corrugated iron sheeting painted in a faded green colour. At each end of these were enormously high sliding doors, again made out of corrugated iron sheeting with a very imperfect fit around the edges which allowed the biting wind to move unimpaired around the interior of the building. The floor was layered with uneven grey concrete scattered with what transpired to be oil stains from the engines of the fleet of antiquated aeroplanes which lived there.

Upon entering the hangars we were met by our two hero parachute instructors, Jim and Brian. Jim was about six foot tall, completely bald, wore serious sunglasses, chewed gum and had an arm in plaster whilst, Brian, listed to the left, had a mop of ginger hair and a speech impediment which resulted in him spraying all and sundry with frothy sputum. He was hobbling about on crutches. This explained the lean to the left, not an encouraging first impression. They justified their condition by relating a recent tale. They had been doing a parachute display using two aircraft and the instructor in the higher aircraft leapt out of his aircraft and went straight through the roof of the lower aeroplane pushing the other instructor out of it. I do believe that neither of them was entirely expecting that sequence of events.

Our first day was to start by jumping around in the hangar, practicing parachute landing falls, PLFs, putting the parachute harness on and off and on again, visiting the conveniences etc., etc. Have I already mentioned the cold on an airfield?

As for the toilet facilities, what can I say? Not only no doors but no bloody roof either! I only mention this because due to a continuous surge of adrenaline over the entire week end I became very familiar with said conveniences.

Anyway, back to the tale, Bradford and I were joined by a varied collection of people who were initially as silent as us. As the morning progressed they started to open up a little more now that we were supposed to be doing things. Slowly people actually started to talk to each other, not normal conversations since we were all still very apprehensive and unsure as to why we were actually doing this at all.

Over the lunch break Bradford and I got chatting to Dick, a seventy year old gentleman who had a previous life in accountancy and wore a grey Beatle haircut; Fiona, a rather attractive willowy young lady with a charming lopsided smile and blond pageboy type hair and Mike, a quietly spoken chubby sort of chap with a lisp. We were never to find out if he had this impediment before the course or as a direct result of the stresses involved. I must admit I had rather taken a fancy to Fiona, although it must be asked why a young lady wearing a young man's hair style could be considered de rigueur. On reflection I believe it covered all bases and propensities. It certainly covered mine I can tell you. The fact was I was becoming increasingly drawn towards her. Sadly it was not being reciprocated. As you might recall, I had a facial palsy. I mention this to try and explain some of the conversations I attempted with Fiona. I asked if she would like to nip off for a drink after our jump? Of course I stated clearly that I meant the parachute jump. She replied with

"You know you mate Bradford, well has he got a girl friend?"

"No I don't think so"

"Do you think he would give me a lift home tonight?"

"Possibly"

"He seems nice, what does he do for a job?"

At this point I blurted out that he was a labourer on a maggot farm and engaged to a super model called Heidi. I couldn't help it, she was slipping away from me into the arms of another who was also my mate to boot. I pondered later that she should have taken pity on someone with palsy. It's not easy, you know, striking up a relationship with an attractive young lady when you can't smile properly, you dribble continuously from the corner of your mouth, you sleep with one eye open and to cap it all your worms don't work. It was shortly afterwards that I noticed these Fiona and Bradford becoming increasingly friendly.

Bastards.

John Clarke

During our general group conversations it was interesting to hear why various people were on the course. Dick thought he was on a philately course, and didn't have the courage to run away, Fiona was doing it for charity and Mike because his fiancé had run off with a skydiver? We all tried to work out the psychology behind that one, I assure you. When Bradford was questioned by the lovely lopsided Fiona about why he was taking part it he merely said because I had suggested it, playing it cool. After further intensive questioning I finally admitted that I was doing it because it I needed diversionary excitement in my life. This statement caused many confused looks, raised eyebrows and an embarrassing silence. But I rescued the situation by saying that I couldn't quite remember why. I don't suppose it was anything to do with my first wife running off with a wrestler. Perhaps Mike and I have more in common than I thought.

Now it was here in that cold bleak desolate place called the hangar, that I earned my reputation as being a very nice, very keen, idiot. We were supposed to practice how to deal with parachuting emergencies, one of which was, what to do if the parachute didn't open. Believe it or not that thought hadn't really occurred to me, up to that point, although quite why does seem a little strange. We would discover if our main parachute had not opened by the highly technical method of looking up and checking with one's eyeballs also feeling no reassuring pressure in one's trousers. Upon discovering this we were to calmly reach down and firmly grab a large metal handle shaped like a letter D. We then had to pull it forcefully (in this situation would there be any other way?) to one side whilst at the same time casting it away, to eventually hit some unfortunate person standing on the ground two thousand

Dunge Bottom

feet below. Right! Now in our practice sessions we were to pretend to throw this handle away and not actually heave it across the hangar.

Adrenaline coursed through my veins and I pulled the metal handle with gusto and with one mighty heave threw it across the room hitting Jim, the instructor, on the temple and flooring him.

He was subsequently removed to the nearest Emergency Department. Apparently I was the only trainee who had ever done this and I am proud to relate that it led to said instructor meeting the female doctor in the Emergency Department who had earlier tended his wounds after the falling out of one aircraft into another aircraft debacle I previously mentioned. I am told that they were reunited like long lost friends and have since built up a very chummy relationship. All's well that ends well... I suppose.

The rest of the first day went a little slower than usual as we were now down to just one instructor. The finale was to actually practice getting in and out of the aircraft whilst wearing our parachutes, helmets and stout boots with the aircraft firmly parked on the ground. I, wrongly as it turned out, assumed that the aircraft in which we were practising was a mock up as it seemed to be of a very flimsy construction, wood, fabric, no seats, oil dripping out of the bottom of both engines, and, when I peered into the cockpit, a huge steering wheel for the pilot to jiggle about. I was, however assured that this was indeed one of the aircraft that we might be using to jump out of. Upon studying it again Bradford and I concluded that it would probably be a good idea to jump out of it anyway should it ever get airborne in the first place. The aircraft in question was a converted 1934 Dragon Rapide. A classic twin engine bi-plane design which was in service with several small airlines of the day and was famous for being able to carry a handful of passengers on short routes across the channel into France and beyond whilst being waited upon by black tie, waistcoated silver service waiters.

Those were the days.

Anyhow, the day we were supposed to do the first jump it was too windy/wet/cold (you will remember that this is normal for airfields, although we didn't realize that at the time), so we were told to keep telephoning the parachuting school every weekend to check to see if the weather conditions were going to be suitable for our first attempt at parachuting. Then we could complete the one jump and get our course certificate.

After what seemed like three months, which actually was only twelve weeks, we were finally told, by the now ritual Sunday morning phone call, to come along because the wind/wet/cold was right. Bugger, it now dawned upon Bradford and me that we might actually have to go and leap out of a perfectly serviceable aircraft after all. This last statement of course uses the expression "perfectly serviceable aircraft" in its broadest possible context. It had been so long since the initial course that we had reached the conclusion that it would never actually happen.

On our original training week end there were about twenty or so people of various sexes and ages and we noticed that only about fifteen of our original group were there that eventful Sunday in January. The aircraft that we used was, as promised, a very similar 1934 De Havilland Rapide only this one had no door in the side merely an enormous great hole. I also noticed a fresh clean looking patch about the size of a man in the roof of the aircraft. "Odd" I mused and thought nothing more of it. I needed all my strength of character to cope with the actuality of getting into the thing in the first place and was far too preoccupied to worry about such petty detail.

Whilst waiting for everyone to get on, I had time to reflect upon my current situation. I admit that the aircraft did remind me of one of the contraptions seen in the film "Those Magnificent Men in Their Flying Machines". It wasn't just not having doors, or the big patch in the roof, but that someone had to go and swing the propellers by hand just to get the engines started. When they did start there were enormous clouds of blue smoke from the exhausts, which we were told was quite normal. That, at least, took my mind off the great big bloody hole in the side.

The plane could seat eight students and the instructor. We all sat on the floor with our well practised devil-may-care expressions, which translated into pale clammy ashen faces and the strong stench of adrenaline. I was so pleased to have got onboard early which meant I could sit up near the front and not next to the hole. I mean if the thing banked sharply to the left there would be a great chance of leaving the aircraft rather too quickly.

Brian, our instructor (the one with the limp) told us all to shuffle on our backsides up towards the front of the aircraft or it wouldn't actually get off the ground, something to do with being overloaded or some such technicality. It would seem that if this type of aircraft has too much weight at the back then it cannot lift the tail up and get the wings at the correct flying angle. All it would do is taxi down the runway at high speed and stay there with no chance of aviation. Eventually we did lift off, touchdown, lift off again, hesitate as to whether to land again or climb away and, oh so slowly, climb up to two thousand feet. We then banked slowly and headed back towards the airfield.

The first student out was a Dick, the aging philatelist,

who had a confused, even bemused, look on his face from the very first moment and whom we were all surprised at seeing again. He did after all have the chance to disappear but, no, he came back. The instructor wisely got him positioned in the open doorway of the aircraft early on, ready for his leap of faith, thinking that he may take time to get ready. Unfortunately when we were about five miles away from the airfield Jim took his eye off the student to give directions to the pilot. Imagine his surprise therefore, when he turned around only to find that the aging Beatle had already exited the aircraft and could now be seen drifting towards the centre of Wolverhampton.

Hey ho plenty more students left.

"How hard can it be to fall out of an aeroplane?" I hear you think. I share your thoughts, it's not as if we haven't practised enough during the training, it really should be quite straightforward. I was going to put all this training into practice right now for the time had come for me to get out of the aircraft. You will, I'm sure, remember that it is a bi-plane with two engines. You are supposed to climb out onto the lower wing and stand behind the port, or left, engine holding onto a wing strut. You then look at Jim who tells you when to let go. Upon receiving the signal you assume the stable spread eagle position and drop. At least, that was the theory. When trying it out in a stationary aircraft on the ground it really was quite easy. What they didn't mention during training is that the aircraft is not on the ground but two thousand feet above it and the airflow behind the engine is over one hundred miles per hour. I will be honest here and admit that this did throw an entirely new perspective on my current situation.

There I am, crouching next to the hole in the side of this string bag of an aircraft looking down into the abyss, with

Dunge Bottom

the wind clutching at me trying to suck me out into oblivion and I am expected to calmly grab hold of the wing strut with my left arm, step out onto the lower wing with my left leg, grasp the strut with my right hand and finally lift my right leg onto the lower wing, all the time expecting to fall through the wing I'm standing on. I then pause and calmly wait for Jim's signal to let go.

What planet are these people on?

As soon as I try and reach out for the wing strut my left hand is ripped backwards by the gale that attacks it, smashing it against the side of the hole. I am at the same time attempting to do all this with my eyes firmly shut. I mean have you ever stood next to a hole in an aircraft and looked down at the ground two thousand feet away? I can tell you it's not a comfortable feeling. After several attempts I now find myself with both arms and both legs firmly crossed with a hundred mile an hour gale hitting my face. I dare to open my eyes at last to glance sideways at Jim, with what I hope is a cool expression on my face only to note what I interpret as a sneer showing on his, damn him. I would at this juncture mention that it is impossible to hear anything above the noise of the engine and the assault by the wind on my feeble battered body. I must rely on my lip reading skills, so I watch his sarcastic mouth for the signal. I wait and wait for it, but nothing comes, I wait a little longer and then decide "oh bugger it" and let go.

During training you are taught to arch your back thus putting you into a stable face down position whilst counting one thousand, two thousand, three thousand, and check. You then cast your gaze upwards to see a fully opened parachute above your head. I chose a different method. Eyes firmly closed and curled up in the foetal position.

Instead of it taking the statutory three seconds for the

John Clarke

parachuteto start to open I had completed my count in less than one nanosecond and was already feverishly looking for the reserve chute's handle when the most appalling pain arose from my left testicle. This was followed by a very rapid spinning into the upright position. "Praise be" I thought. The parachute had opened properly and I was alive, albeit in pain. Vision was proving difficult but continuously wiping the tears away from my eyes helped. This was the moment to relax and enjoy the fabulous experience. I could see for miles. To my right were the Welsh mountains, to my left the city of Wolverhampton lay sprawled out like the concrete conurbation that it truly is. It was January and there was a strange yellowy brown coloured air hanging over the city, not overly attractive actually. I made a mental note to check about air pollution if I was to do this more often. A thought then occurred to me which took me by surprise, especially since tears were still pouring down my face and my left testicle now seemed to be on fire! At sometime soon I would be arriving at the airfield , this was the plan anyway. The problem was that I couldn't actually see it. "Tricky" I thought. "Still not to worry, can't be that difficult". After a few moments I changed my plans and began to panic

"Where the bloody hell is this airfield?" Must try to stay calm, control my breathing get it down to forty breaths a minute. That's better, hang on though what is that little dot down there. Brilliant it's a twin engine bi plane and what is it doing. Stopping!"

Even for an air related ignoramus, I realized that airplanes don't just stop, it must have landed and where do airplanes land? At airfields. Fantastic I've found it where it was all along: underneath me.

Who ever thought of looking down?

Dunge Bottom

I did think, at the time, that the instructors needed to cover this area more thoroughly in their training, after all three hundred and fifty acres of grass runways, hangars and aircraft are not always immediately obvious to the tyro parachutist. I pledged to write to them about this later.

My mind began to drift, alternating between exquisite pain and the freedom of flight. After a while something began to intrude into my reveries, a faint mewing call, a buzzard perhaps? Possibly a stormy petrel? How wonderful is nature? The cry became a little louder and dare I say more insistent. Not really a bird's cry now, more of a mammalian type grunting. "Do they have foxes or musk on airfields?" I thought, surely a safety issue here. I began to wander off again and then more clearly I heard;

"Left toggle, left toggle you stupid bastard!"

I looked around and saw nothing then, being a quick learner, I remembered to look down. "Bugger", I had forgotten that when you get nearer the ground they shout at you with a megaphone telling you which string to pull to steer yourself so that you can land into wind. The Bastard was me and the ground was coming up to meet me very quickly indeed. "Now then Clarke" I thought, "remember your training."

"Look at the horizon, bend your knees and collapse sideways rolling over onto your side and shoulders absorbing the impact gradually. Easy Peasy."

I looked down. The ground was close and approaching speedily. I straightened my legs to reach for the ground and landed in a crumpled heap finishing about eighteen inches below ground level. I firmly believed that every bone in my body was broken and it had felt nothing like falling off the wooden box we had practiced in training. Nor was I sure that my teeth are as firmly fixed as they once were.

John Clarke

"For Christs sake you couldn't 'ave done any worse if you tried" screeched this voice, still, I noted, through the megaphone even though the instructor was a foot away from me. Normally I would have remonstrated with him, pointing out that I could have done much worse if I had really put my mind to it, except I was completely winded and unable to speak at all, moving was also a problem. Another man in a Land Rover kindly came and got me, returning me to the hangar and unceremoniously dumping me off at the door.

Later when we had chance to exchange experiences, I found that the group had mixed success with their first jump, mine being one of the more successful attempts, as I had actually found the airfield! Apparently the aging Beatle had landed in one of the main streets of Wolverhampton and was currently being interviewed by the local constabulary under the Terrorism Act 1975, Bradford had landed in the middle of the roundabout at the entrance of the airfield causing a car, two push bikes and a mobility scooter to have some sort of altercation. A third had missed the airfield altogether and gone straight through the side of a market garden greenhouse. It would appear that his outline was clearly visible through the glass sides of the greenhouse like a scene from a Tom & Jerry cartoon. Mike had actually landed on a hangar roof, which being made of asbestos was not keen on supporting his weight. He went through the roof and was heading for the concrete floor when the lines of his chute caught up in the steelwork leaving him dangling three feet above the floor drooling gently and emitting a low moaning sound. It was also noted by casual observers that there appeared to be a pool of ooze directly beneath our parachutist hero. Nobody quite had the bravery to check on the ooze and kindly decided that it must have been on the floor before his arrival. I believe another had made an even worse landing attempt than I and had put his legs out horizontally just before impact and landed completely on his arse. He was on his way to the Emergency Department with a suspected impacted haemorrhoid. Fiona, the lovely lopsided young lady whom Bradford had impressed during our training, had deposited herself in one of the filter beds of the adjacent sewage works. Surprisingly few were keen to go and rescue her apart from Bradford of course.

Sometime later I would have the chance to attempt a rescue of a damsel in distress myself. I had the, not entirely noble, idea that she might find her new super hero (me) the love of her life and ignore the palsy. She had unfortunately landed in a tree and was stuck there. I bravely called up to her not to worry as I was here now and everything would be fine. She smiled down at me and I saw her fear lighten as I climbed the tree to help her. Actually she was higher up in this tree than appeared from the ground but eventually I got to an adjacent branch where I stood with my left arm wrapped around the tree trunk with my other arm fully extended towards her. It was rather like a scene from a Tarzan movie where Tarzan swings through trees from branch to branch, reaches out with his muscled arms and grasps the wrist of the forlorn female. With a smooth powerful heave he pulls her up to safety and into his arms. The lady can do no more than swoon before his perfect manliness. So, very much in the same vein, I grabbed her wrist, smiling lopsidedly and drooling. She smiled back and started to edge closer to me and sanctuary.

I refer you to the film scene mentioned above and would comment that in real life, it's bollocks, for just as she neared the tree, me and safety she slipped and fell, I duly let go of

John Clarke

her wrist, whereupon she plummeted onto another large branch with her legs opened. Her screams indicated some level of discomfort as she rotated round the branch and turned completely upside down. At this point gravity worked and she continued falling to ground level, landing on her head. No chance of going out for a drink then?

Bradford and I attended the parachuting events twice more before we realised that the attrition rate was far too high and we were the only remaining survivors of our initial group. Sadly Bradford decided to bail out of our adventures at this point as he was becoming increasingly preoccupied with the rather lovely, willowy, lopsided Fiona.

On reflection, my second jump was even scarier than the first. It was patiently explained to me by the instructor, who listed to the left, that it was because I now knew exactly what was going to happen. The kind understanding person with the megaphone, who sympathetically referred to me as "Bastard", described my efforts this time as even worse. I was unsure as to whether to consider this a compliment or not. After all how could it be worse than the first? I explained that on my virgin jump I had looked down, pointed my toes at the ground, didn't roll onto my side, didn't listen to his instructions on the megaphone, all cardinal sins I am led to believe. "What could be worse?" I asked

"You turned up" he said grinning venomously.

Reflecting on the experience I did try to twist things into a positive light and decided I should try one more jump, after all it can't be that hard to start to make progress can it? I can now reveal that, according to all the instructors including the chief jumpmaster, I was the worst student that they had ever had. They seemed to take great delight in confirming this to me at the debriefing session following my

Dunge Bottom

latest jump.

How proud I felt at this point.

"Wow, that's something to impress the ladies with" thought I.

"Hang on a minute, did they say the worst and what ladies?"

"The bastards."

Could I really have been that bad? In my mind I ran through the correct sequence of events and actions before during and after a parachute jump and after much consideration felt that I had to agree with them as I really didn't do anything correctly.

Things got worse for now they also took great delight in telling me that before I jumped for the third time, they would make me pack my own parachute. I could not believe it. It took me numerous attempts to get this enormous piece of material to fit into the bag at all. If you have ever tried to get any item back into its packaging you will sympathise. It is the same with a parachute, except ten times as difficult. Also the whole thing is held in place with elastic bands. Not your aircraft quality type, the sort you could comfortably bungee jump with, oh no, more the sort you got from Woolworths. No wonder I was an even more nervous wreck, no wonder, therefore, that this impacted on my performance.

It would be impossible to be more frightened than I was before the third jump. So with some hesitation and deep regret I decided the time had come to adopt plan, "Romeo Alpha"...... Run away. I must admit that with the advantage of hindsight and the passing of time I very much enjoyed the experience but perhaps it wasn't quite the right thing for me. Still, I was glad I tried it. Additionally, in the days following the jumps I experienced appalling pain in both

24

John Clarke

testicles, which caused much amusement to the casual observer watching my perambulations. I strongly believe that due to this experience, my testicles made a firm commitment, henceforth, to be worn internally at all times, as they certainly did not wish to repeat such an appalling episode in their lives!

3

The Future?

"**W**hat the bloody hell is that?" I spluttered out loud to anyone who cared to listen. It was a beautiful mid July day and I was walking along the public footpath from the Izaak Walton Hotel to Ilam in the beautiful southern part of the Peak District. That lunchtime my intention was nothing more than to get to the village and there I would sit by the river that flowed through the centre of it, enjoy a refreshing ice cream and, if I felt particularly daring, a flake. My expression of surprise was due to the fact that I noticed a multicoloured contraption high up on the hillside to my right. It was triangular shaped and mainly red white and blue. I really couldn't make it out. "What on earth is it?" I asked myself. Suddenly it picked itself up to reveal a man underneath who started to run down the distant, steep grassy slope towards me, seemingly without effort. After a short distance the two left the ground and took to the sky.

Dunge Bottom

There was a loud flapping noise coming from it as the contraption rapidly descended, along with its attendant man, down into the field where I stood watching, my mouth wide open in complete amazement. They collided with the ground with only the slightest stumbling from the male form hanging underneath.

I could not help it. My curiosity was in overdrive as I ran towards him. "Bloody hell, that was incredible" I greeted the alien creature before me. "What on earth is it?"

The man looked at me in what I interpreted as being an ever so slightly condescending way before he replied:

"A Hang Glider"

"Bloody hell" I reiterated. I was immediately enthralled by what I had just seen. So enthralled, in fact, that I just had to ask him the obvious question.

"Are you in much testicular pain?"

After my parachuting, it was a subject close to my heart, not to mention the other bits, and it was a genuine question, but to my dismay my new flying friend beat a hasty retreat. "Never mind" I thought, "This is worth a closer look."

I could think of nothing better than doing a bit of finding out about what I had seen, so off to the public library.

It's amazing what one can glean from the Readers Digest Book of Early Flying. For example,

I came very quickly to realize that anyone involved in pioneering aviation just had to have a silly name, for example, Mr Bernoulli, Percy Pilcher, Otto Lillienthal and one of my favourites, Sir George Cayley.

Now Sir George was a member of the landed gentry back in the 1800s, whose land happened to include a big high and wide valley. He decided after much thought, and Port, that air and water are both fluids therefore a boat should sail through the air so he and his coachman built a wooden

John Clarke

sailing type boat with the sail. Instead of being vertical like a boat was put horizontally and also had an oar sticking out of the back to steer it. Taking off could prove problematical so he put it on a wheeled trolley type of affair.

One sunny April day, with a gentle breeze blowing across and up one side of his valley he and his coachman harnessed up a couple of his staunchest horses and dragged his flying machine up to the top of the valley side, some three hundred feet above the valley floor. Now, with the contraption facing into the wind and down the valley side, all he needed was a pilot.

As you may have gathered by now, Sir George was a highly intelligent chap, having realized this air water fluid business, so intelligent that he wouldn't even dream of trying it himself, so...his coachman was instructed to climb aboard. Initially fearing more for his employment than his life he very reluctantly climbed aboard and was launched out into the abyss. Surprisingly or perhaps not he did survive as the aircraft did successfully fly and land safely in the valley floor. Legend has it that upon landing he dismounted the flying machine, and disappeared into the distance at high speed, presumably now expecting further commands to commit aviation.

He was never seen again.

As I read on I discovered more about these strange characters from the past and I cannot go on without mentioning what I learnt about Mr. Bernoulli. Daniel Bernoulli was a product of a genius family. His father, Johann, was Chair of Mathematics at Groningen University and his uncle was Jacob Bernoulli an equally famous mathematician. Unfortunately they did seem to be a rather dysfunctional family as Jacob and Johann hated each other and spent most of their lives trading mathematical insults

Dunge Bottom

that, frankly, most normal people did not understand.

There was also tension between Daniel and his father. Johann Bernoulli wanted his son to study philosophy and logic before going into medicine. Daniel did all this, completing his doctorate in 1738, however, on the quiet, he was also indulging his passion for...mathematics and physics, the scamp.

Daniel eventually became interested in hydrodynamics and his major work, Hydrodynamica was published in 1738. It explained what became known as Bernoulli's Principle which has enormous relevance to those of us who fly. Sadly, his incredible success (he was awarded the Grand Prize of the Paris Academy ten times) caused a terrible rift between him and his father. They were joint winners of the prize in 1738 and Johann was furious that his son was considered his equal. It was a jealousy that poisoned their relationship for the rest of their lives. Both men towered over Europe as geniuses of the mathematical and physical sciences and yet they could not speak to each other as father and son. Had it happened today, it could have been the most boring Jerry Springer show ever.

So there I was having discovered some of the history but still at a loss as to how these things actually fly. I felt this was something I ought to make efforts to understand before strapping myself underneath one. The 'My First Book of Flight', at least I think that was the title, threw some light on the subject. In very simple terms, my favourite sort, it explained the link between the principles of Mr Bernoulli and, say, a Boeing 747 which when fully loaded weighs approximately three hundred and fifty tons. You see, if I could understand how a Boeing flew I would feel a lot more confident that a wing could carry my weight I was, after all, only eight stones. Now I know a lot of people consider it to be the eighty thousand pounds of thrust from the four enormous engines that make the plane commit aviation and to a degree they are correct. However, four jumbo sized engines would be impractical for hang gliding and so logic dictates there must be other factors at play. Furthermore, what would happen should those mighty Pratt and Whitneys or Rolls Royce engines actually stop at thirty five thousand feet? Incidentally, I would remind readers that this event has actually happened on more than one occasion. This has resulted in screaming from the passengers inside, much spilling of concessionary G&Ts and such words as "Jeepers" and "Ooh heck" from the flight deck. Fortunately the aircraft would turn into the world's largest glider and as a consequence be able to land safely, assuming there was an airfield or very large field within range.

"Impossible" is the cry from you, the assembled reader, and without Mr. Bernoulli you would be correct.

You see he discovered the principles of flight, the primary one being, how a wing produces lift, to support, in our case, three hundred and fifty tons of metal and humanity. What Mr. B, decided was as follows...

Take a box of air, it is full of air molecules (small bits of stuff – refer to physics text books or Stephen Fry for further detailed definition.)Now you need to imagine a box of air big enough to hold a Boeing 747. As the aircraft wings move through the air, molecules obviously flow over and under the wing surfaces. Now here is the cunning bit, the top surface of the wing is curved. This means that the molecules that flow over the top surface have further to go than those underneath. To make his ideas work fully Bernoulli now needed to come up with the theory of constancy. This means that everything tries to remain in its comfort zone, as they are happy where they are – therefore if a molecule is moved from its particular place in the box it would very much like to go back there again. So with that nugget of information, back to the wings bit.

You still remember the law of constancy? Well, when the two molecules at the very front of the wing are split up, one going over the top and the other going underneath, it is natural for them to want to arrive at the back of the wing at the same time. So the only way it can happen is if the one that goes over the top travels faster because it has further to go. This has the effect of stretching the gap between the molecules on the top surface, which in turn reduces the pressure on top of the wing surface, because there are exactly the same number of molecules top and bottom; and you'll never guess............

This sucks the wing upwards da da!!!

Now Mr. Newton (the falling apple man) plays a part here because he said each action has an equal and opposite reaction, i.e., if I punch you in the nose then you punch me back again. So in addition to the suck, the wing is also angled upwards at the front which deflects the air hitting it underneath downwards, therefore again helping to push the wing upwards. To sum up, when we fly the aircraft is both sucked and pushed upwards at the same time. If this appears at all confusing, can I suggest that you try a couple of practical experiments to prove it.

Experiment 1

Take a spoon hold it by the end of the handle vertically downwards and place it under a running tap. As the water flows around the bowl of the spoon you will see that the spoon moves sideways = LIFT.

Experiment 2

Take a piece of paper, hold it by the narrow end and let it hang down. Place your mouth near the edge you are holding and blow gently over the top of the paper. Surprise, surprise you will note that the bottom edge of the paper now starts to lift up towards the edge you are holding = LIFT.

So next time you fly away in the great silver bird in the sky may I humbly request that you offer a prayer up to the amazing Mr. Bernoulli, the father of Suck!!

Hang Gliding with Oomie

I quickly discovered that getting started at this hang gliding lark was not as easy as it sounded. I had found out how the things work but could not find anyone who knew anything about it. Further investigation also proved difficult. You see there was no internet then, the ether hadn't been invented and it was very much a trip on the bus to WHSmith and then spending time

scouring the magazine section for any likely looking stuff to satiate my unswerving quest for information on how to actually get into the air.

After much going to libraries and scanning copies of the Yellow Pages I found a hang gliding school in Brighton and a local club based in Derby. I sent for the details from the Brighton school and I was immediately put off by the picture of the Instructor. He had less control of his hair than me, a beard you could hide a badger in and, to cap it all, smoked a pipe. No way was I going there, after all street , or should that be hill credibility, was important to a young man in the seventies and a pipe was not "hip". Incidentally, the five hundred mile return journey was also a disincentive. Nevertheless I desperately needed something to shine at. After all here I was divorced, crap job and only half a face that works. It was not the happiest of positions and

Dunge Bottom

parachuting was never going to be a career option! The Derby club seemed a little more hopeful but the contact was unavailable apparently due to a short stay in hospital. I understood he was due to be released soon however.

It was at that point that lady luck smiled on the boy Clarke (for a change) As unbelievable as it sounds I happened to meet a bloke called Des, in a pub, who actually had a hang glider in his garage and he would swap it for my Nikon camera. What was even better, his brother had a friend who once saw someone hang glide and would phone me and tell me how to do it. "Brilliant" I thought, "how can I refuse help of this calibre?" I was tremendously excited and at the first opportunity I drove over to Stoke-on-Trent to pick up the glider. It was longer than I expected it to be, about twenty feet and it looked like a rolled up carpet wrapped up in tatty clear polythene sheeting. To be honest it looked a bit dodgy but I was reassured by Des that it was okay. A bag for it cost more so he thought he would save a bit by not buying one, "fair enough" I thought. He told me it was a Skyhook 3A. Apparently the "A" was very important but I was unable to ascertain why. I made a mental note to find out later. On a technical note, I later discovered that the A meant it had a bit of string (aircraft quality of course) tied to various bits on top of the glider whilst the Skyhook 3 didn't. The sum total of my diligent research.

I couldn't wait to put it together, so the very next evening I was to be found on our back lawn trying to build it. I later learned that the correct terminology is "rigging it". It was bigger than I thought and red and white, shaped like a triangle with several bits of shiny aluminium tubing dotted about, all held together with steel wires. You know, I had the horrible feeling that like the old bi plane it would be bits of string stopping it falling apart. Well actually the bits of string were saved for the top of the glider. I considered the reasons for their presence and concluded that it was probably a weight saving design feature to improve the aerodynamic efficiency. It's amazing the bollocks you'll try and sell to yourself, to control fear and stop running away. Putting it together was interesting on two counts, firstly the lawn wasn't big enough, causing not inconsiderable damage to my mother's prize buddleias and secondly because we did seem to have some bits left over. Des said that he thought that the bits were spares but as he had never flown it himself he wasn't completely sure. I was a little dubious as some of the spares consisted of nuts and bolts which, of course, normally hold things together. I assumed that one would want everything held together in-flight. On closer inspection it wasn't obvious where there might be some missing on the rigged glider, so I crossed my fingers and decided that all was satisfactory. Anyway it looked okay, which was the main thing. I had now got a photograph of a hang glider which I pinched out of a magazine and my new acquisition did look similar, apart from the colours, of course. I had never noticed before but the glider also had a sort of swing seat which connected to somewhere underneath the glider with an aluminium hook. I later found out this was called a carabiner. A climbing friend of mine told me that these aluminium hook things were used a lot in climbing and helped stop climbers falling off cliffs. I took this as most encouraging. I actually thought that you hung by your armpits, so having a seat seemed to make things really easy. I also spoke on the phone to Des' brother about how to fly the glider. It seemed very straight forward; apparently what you have to do is…

1. Put it together, strap the seat on around your bum, pick the whole thing up.

Dunge Bottom

2. Run down the hill until you take off.

Easy!

He was a little bit vague about what to do next but he did say, reassuringly, that the landing did seem to happen naturally. I could not wait until Saturday when I had a free day to try it out.

In the meantime I spoke to a mate of mine called Oomie. I told him what I was planning and he seemed very keen to come along and try his luck as well. Oomie, was a cheerful soul with a ready smile and lived next door to Bradford who, he informed me, was getting engaged to lopsided Fiona. No wonder I've not heard much from him lately...bastard.

"I think I can help" said Oomie.

"How so?" I questioned.

"I saw something on telly about hang gliding about a year ago"

"Can't refuse an offer like that" I replied.

We arranged to meet at the public toilets near Thorpe in Derbyshire, a small quiet limestone village perched at the foot of Thorpe Cloud and at the entrance to Dovedale, a famous beauty spot known for steep hills and winds that prevailed (over what I wasn't quite sure). More relevant to our needs, it had a small gravelled car park adjacent to the village post office, boasting aforementioned brand new public toilets.

I had spotted what looked to be a great hill to start with just behind the car park. I recced it and it seemed perfect; smoothish grass, quite steep with just a few medium sized rocks sticking up and about one hundred and fifty feet high, the hill, not the sticky up rocks. I was told by a local that it was usually called the rifle range and be careful when the red flag is flying. I wasn't completely sure why and he didn't elucidate further. It looked great, but I have to admit I had slight misgivings about the sticky rocks, still I didn't think it would be too much of a problem as we would be flying way above them. I was early to bed as Oomie and I planned to meet at nine the next morning. I took some Imodium later, and wondered if I'd picked up a bug as my stomach wasn't quite right. Still, I wasn't going to let it spoil the day.

The day dawned bright and sunny and we drew straws as to who was going first and damn it, Oomie won. Carefully following our brief, we assembled the glider. We still had one or two bits left over, although different bits this time but we did not worry about such detail as it couldn't possibly have any significance. I carefully strapped the seat around the top of Oomie's thighs and then unstrapped the seat from around Oomie's thighs because we were at the bottom of the hill. We quickly figured out that to fly down, you have to be at the top. We carried the glider up the hill. By heck that was hard work, not only were we going uphill but the blasted wind seemed to be pushing us down the hill at the same time. This was not fun.

It was great view from the top of our hill, a narrow valley led away on the right down to the stepping stones at Dovedale, still a famous beauty spot, where the river Dove gently cascaded through a majestic tree-lined limestone gorge before spewing out into a wide-open valley and joining the river Manifold. In fact when the wind was in the right direction I could hear the river tinkling and gurgling as it passed over weirs, and around boulders left strewn in the river bed by the last ice age, when the whole area was sculpted by the retreat of the glaciers. As I listened I realized that the sound was funnelled up the valley sides and amplified as it entered the natural amphitheatre before our

Dunge Bottom

hill, a truly fabulous sight and one which inevitably attracts tourists.

Immediately in front of me was the flat topped hill called Thorpe Cloud which is about five hundred feet high and all of about three hundred yards away with an open rolling grass field to the left returning towards the car park.

There were lots of small fluffy cauliflower shape clouds gently drifting across the azure sky casting fleeting shadows across the emerald green pasture below,

"Ah how beautiful". I spoke dreamily to Oomie as he sat looking back and forth from the spare parts to the glider with a thoughtful expression on his face. I will be honest with you here, it was something of a ruse to try and delay our first foray into the world of pioneering aviation, as I was becoming somewhat nervous. As I looked down I silently admitted to myself that the hill did look a lot steeper from the top than it did from the bottom. Those rocks also appeared to have bred as there were definitely more there now than when we arrived. However, Oomie had now strapped the seat around his thighs, nice and tight, don't want to fall out now do we? Whilst on the subject of safety, we had taken into consideration the fact that some bodily damage may occur during our early attempts. To that end we had adopted the use of stout pit boots with toe protection, as we were sure that hitting one of these large sticky up rocks could cause a nasty stubbed toe. Strong gloves were also the order of the day, protecting us from nasty thistle barbs. We had almost thought of everything, but not quite. It was Oomie's mum who had, on hearing of her son's plans to fly, enquired about a crash helmet. Initially not something we had considered but upon reflection it seemed appropriate. Luckily I had one that I used previously in my motorcycle racing days. It was

John Clarke

affectionately described as a pudding basin, because, well, if you envisage a round pudding basin (one that you would use to bake a pudding) and attach straps to it, then that is exactly what it would look like.

I had previously acquired this particular helmet because I wanted to emulate my motorbike racing hero, Percy Tait, who used to race Triumph Bonnevilles wearing the same sort of skid lid. Mind you I don't think it ever looked as good on me as it did on Percy. I did once meet the great man at Mallory Park a racing circuit in Leicestershire when I was racing a sidecar outfit. An outfit being a lowered motorbike on the right hand side of a three foot wide platform (chair) with a small fairing at the front with a grab handle on which the passenger sat.

It was raining very hard and I was the passenger on my mates sidecar, powered by a 650cc race-prepared Bonneville engine. Being passenger meant moving about all over the place during cornering, because as we went around a right hand bend the rear wheel of the bike would tend to lift off the ground which resulted in a loss of traction so I needed to get up and lean with all my weight over the back wheel to keep it on the track and maintain acceleration. Conversely when going around a left hand bend the flat chair I lay on started to lift up so I needed to lean right out as far as possible over the track to keep it down and stop the whole thing turning over. In this particular race we were nearing the end and placed third which was highly unusual for us I can assure you, most of the time I rebuilt the engine after every race as it generally blew up around lap five or six. We approached the sharp right hand hairpin at Mallory where I was leaning hard over the back wheel, then accelerated through the bend and entered the straight where I needed to then let go of the

Dunge Bottom

bike and dive forward lying flat on the chair. This was where it all went wrong. Due to the torrential rain the aluminium platform was streaming with water. I was wearing shiny black and dare I say rather sexy leathers and made a leap to grab the safety handle at the front of the chair. I missed and, as the machine accelerated away, I gracefully slid off the back of the outfit and lay face down on the race track. Luckily everyone coming up behind managed to miss me. But I had the embarrassment of trotting along the track to catch up with my rider who had stopped just around the next bend and was kind enough to wait for me. The largest crowd at this circuit assembled at the hairpin and I was given the most tumultuous applause by them. I was not asked to participate again, shame really. Never mind, back to the hang gliding.

With a look of steely determination Oomie put on the pudding basin picked up the glider, gave a maniacal laugh…and ran. I have to say I was expecting a little in the way of preparation and psyching oneself up, but no, he just went. I must also admit I thought I heard a degree of undecipherable mutterings as he ran like a sprinter bursting from the starting blocks. He managed three steps before he fell over and stopped. His face following his belly into the dandelion covered slope. As he did so he generated an impressive cloud of dust and flora. Like all good crash investigators we conducted a comprehensive post mortem (not literally of course) and decided that strapping the seat quite so tightly around the thighs was a mistake as it effectively hobbled Oomie and made it impossible for him to run. He also confirmed that everything was fine until he picked the glider up and looked down the hill. Still we expected a steep learning curve so Oomie dusted himself off and tried again. This attempt was truly awesome.

John Clarke

Oomie started his run, perhaps understandably, a little tentatively. Picking up speed he managed to accelerate very quickly indeed and disappeared down the hill like a cheese being rolled at one of those festivals in Dorset where everyone chases it and ends up in hospital, except for the poor sod that ends up winning a slightly battered cheese. At any moment, I thought, he will be airborne and my dreams of flight would come true...well for him anyway.

Oomie got approximately halfway down the hill when he let out a scream and accelerated to an even faster rate. It really was impressive. I'm sure I couldn't run that fast and Oomie had not got the body of a sprinter, more perhaps a junior sumo wrestler, squat, broad, fat bellied, "looks certainly can be deceiving" I thought. When he reached the bottom of the hill, still running, I realised that maybe something was not quite right about this, particularly as at this point he simply fell over generating yet another enormous cloud of dust and dung. This caused some alarm to the large flock of sheep who had previously produced said excrement. To add insult to injury that wind, which oddly seemed stronger now, got him from behind and blew the whole thing over so he was now suspended off the ground and wrapped around one of the aluminium bits of the glider. I slithered down to him as quickly as I could, hoping that the metal bits on the glider were still straight. When I arrived at our stricken craft I couldn't help but notice that there was a degree of moaning and swearing from the bat like creature that was still suspended upside down like one of the beetles I used to flip when I was a kid. I did also hear a sharp snapping sound as the bits of string on the top of the glider decided to break and the whole thing collapsed gently onto the ground, causing more expletives from Oomie whose head had buried itself at an unnatural angle in the dirt.

I tried to console him but to no avail. He was becoming rather cross now and I certainly did not want have his ire directed towards myself, after all he did have the attributes of a sumo wrestler.

When I had untangled him and set him straight on the ground a more detailed debriefing took place as we retied the broken bits of string. Oomie too, was surprised at how quickly he went down the hill and confirmed that running that fast was indeed quite straightforward as gravity works and he couldn't actually slow down even if he had wanted to.

"How about if we wait for a bit more wind before you try again" I ventured. This innocent comment triggered a further lengthy discussion as to why it wasn't now my turn. I won however, as after all he was on a roll and wouldn't want to lose the flow now would he? Back at the top of the hill he once again prepared for action. Fortunately the wind had strengthened and was now nicely trying to push the glider down the hill.

"Just right" I said "now you really will be able to run very quickly indeed and finally commit aviation!

I couldn't help but admire his confidence in me. I mean his attempts so far were a little disappointing and he was I'm sure beginning to collect some bruising as well as deeply ingrained sheep poo.

"Let's get the show on the road" he muttered, Oomie was an aficionado of the worst of American action movie clichés.

It was difficult not to notice that we now had an audience, a group of six ramblers who were volunteering well meaning advice – some of which appeared to possibly have some merit. Anyway, Oomie didn't run as far this time, on account of the wind, I think. He took six or seven really good strides and slipped on the dung causing him to fall backwards. His momentum not being impeded by this catastrophic event he slid the remaining hundred feet down the hill on his arse at the same time being given extra propulsion by the ever increasing wind.

What impressed me the most was how managed to miss all the rocks. Well nearly all the rocks because he did kind of hit one near the bottom which was lucky because it stopped him going any further. The downside to this was, as I discovered when I once again reached him, was that his jacket, shirt and tee shirt and been neatly cut all the way down his back with just the slightest of red lines showing on his skin. "Perhaps if we had more wind or you ran longer next time?" I sympathetically enquired of the prostrate pilot. It was at that moment he decided, very emphatically I thought, that it was now my turn to try.

Once again back at the top on looking down the rock strewn slope, we noticed that our audience had now grown with a group of Scouts joining the ramblers as well as two highland cattle. A pre-flight briefing then took place between all the assembled throng, excluding the two highland cattle of course, and one or two good ideas started to emerge. The most thought provoking were:

"Were we sure the glider was pointing the right way round?" This from one of the ramblers, we gleefully showed him the copy of the photo we had previously acquired.

"Was the glider too heavy?" How the hell should we know?

"What about a steeper hill?" Interesting that one, we'll keep that in reserve.

Now I was built like lean clean mean fighting machine as I survived almost exclusively on Mars Bars and lemonade in those days and was sure that I could run faster than my

Dunge Bottom

Sumo chum so I was more than confident as I attached myself to my aircraft. The seat straps did actually feel quite uncomfortable and could possibly hinder running, also the crash helmet kept being pushed over my eyes by the rope of the harness as it ran up the back of my neck. As I stood at the top of the hill I suddenly noticed that there were definitely more rocks about, and the hill was definitely much steeper now (seemingly vertical) and on looking further afield into the expected landing zone I couldn't help notice that a family of four were joining our ever increasing audience and what was worse they were starting a picnic right there where I was going to land. How stupid could people be? I called out to them gesticulating in the hope of showing them the error of their ways.

"We just wanted to be near the crash," the father joked refusing to move to a safer area. "And you won't get this far anyway."

"Right" I thought pulling the basin harder on to my head, quietly determined to prove them wrong.

"Control breathing that's the first priority, heart rate now settling, flatulence increasing, beginning to sweat a little now" I took a deep breath closed eyes and ran.

As soon as I started to move I felt the wind propelling me from behind, "Brilliant" I thought…briefly as the rope tipped the crash helmet forward over my eyes again.

"Bugger"

This was not the only thought that passed through my mind as I was hurtling down this steep dung covered, rock strewn slope at a speed I was not actually capable of and completely blind. "How would I know if I had taken off ?" I was still clinging on to the expectation of flight. Also, and this could be assumed to be ridiculously optimistic, "how would I know when I had landed as well?"

John Clarke

As it turned out I never did know if I took off (witnesses from the Park Rangers department, now also assembled, declared that at no time did my feet leave the ground) but landing was immediately apparent as I ran into flat ground at the bottom, at terminal velocity, my momentum of course carried me on following the gradient of the hill whilst my feet moved horizontally and consequently my legs buckled under me and I arrived in crumpled heap in front of the family of picnickers. The father was sympathetic whilst letting me know that he was right all along and his family was quite safe where they were…smart arse.

Right, drink break. Oomie and I had some serious thinking to do here, after all, we were here to fly, or so I thought. Many theories were expounded now by the large assembly of people which included the police and fire service who arrived with sirens blaring and blue lights flashing. Our brave attempts had been reported by a well meaning member of the public as an air crash.

The latest wheeze proffered by our appreciative audience was to try and tie rocks to us for extra ballast, that way we would definitely go down that bloody hill even quicker. We were too involved in our debate to pay heed when one of the small picnicking children muttered about why was such a pretty red flag now flying at the top of the hill, our minds were on other more weighty things.

When we, once again, reached the top of the hill we could not help but notice the occasional zinging, whistling, high pitched noise playing over the wind. This coincided with occasional puffs of earth and rock. To my disappointment I saw that the assembled masses at the bottom of the hill were quickly withdrawing. I couldn't quite hear what they were saying, "but no matter" I thought. I was just psyching myself up again when Oomie mentioned the

Dunge Bottom

sudden lack of "zinging". To our consternation we were joined by a rotund, red faced gentleman who seemed to have difficulty both breathing and speaking (it was a very steep hill you will remember). He was wearing a tweed jacket, breeches and a hat, and who seemed displeased to see us there. He sat down, then lay down, then sat back up again and commenced swearing at us, muttering something about:

"Who the effin ell were we, what the effin ell were we doin' 'ere, didn't we effin see the effin flag, and did we want to be effin killed 'cos the effin ricochets from the adjacent rifle range would certainly effin do it if we effin stayed there any effin longer."

There was quite a long pause for breath whilst we took on board what he was saying, internalised it and synthesised it into our action plan. The tweedy chap had now recovered his breath and before he could launch off into another tirade we decided to carry the glider down the hill. You can imagine the ignominy of it. After all, we had carried the bloody thing up there and now we had to carry it down as well! We did get a little concerned when this now less red faced but still rotund gentleman followed us down the hill demanding his "Effin fifty pence flying fee."

Yet more ignominy!

At this point we started to become a little incensed and began to remonstrate with the cherry faced fool about this obvious attempt at extortion and that we were seriously considering calling upon the services of the local constabulary.

Further explosive noises emanated from this verbose individual who amongst other things pointed that he actually owned the "Effin land" we had been playing on.

A hasty retreat seemed the order of the day.

46

John Clarke

Later, in the pub Oomie and I decided that the park ranger was right we needed a bigger hill...

"I know just where there is one" I proudly announced to my chum. It was the six hundred foot monster called Bunster, where I had first seen someone fly off and was near the village of Ilam which was just down the road. "John, you are brilliant" I thought to myself. It was at this point that a somewhat subdued Oomie mentioned that he now needed to go home as he was naked from the waist up due to his upper garments being ripped off his back, "fair enough" I agreed, the beer having restored my sense of reason. We agreed to meet at the new monster the following Saturday and try again.

To my consternation, a week later Oomie telephoned to tell me he couldn't make it, something about having to go emergency shopping with his girlfriend Caroline. Actually it was quite strange because Oomie and I never quite managed to meet up again to go hang gliding, strange business, hey ho never mind. In fact in the years following the subject of our hang gliding adventurers was neatly side stepped by him and I was never sure why?

Saturday again dawned bright, sunny and this time smelly as well. I'd had that bit of a tummy bug come back in the night. I resolved to monitor what I was eating in case there was a pattern developing. Well, there I was at the top of this bloody great big hill, I mean it was bloody enormous. I could see the village of Ilam dimly through the mist off to the left. Immediately below me and slightly left was a big pond surrounded by high trees, whilst behind me were two big fields. Quite disconcertingly, further behind and below, was my flat topped hill of last week. The wind was quite strong and blew straight into my face. I frowned at this added complication.

Dunge Bottom

"I won't be able to run so hard if the wind is blowing at me" I thought.

"Right Clarke here goes, I'll just try it once and that'll do I think then I can move on to the next thing. Hells teeth I can't run, this bloody wind is just too strong, I............. Oh Lord!"

I could not run because my feet were not actually on the ground. More pertinent, there was an intense pain in my testicles. Why did anything to do with aviation prove to be such a ball ache? The seat straps were digging in and

"Oh no I'm going blind as well – I can't see!" I'd forgotten to do something about the rope and the helmet slipped over my eyes again.

Despite all the distractions it was an incredible experience, for all of a sudden there I was six hundred feet off the ground, completely blind, with excruciating testicular pain.

"Shit what do I do?"

It was at this moment I realized that all my previous efforts had been towards getting off the ground, little thought had gone into what to do in the air. The weakness in my thinking was now only too apparent! Actually being blind helped here. Since I couldn't see anything it would make it difficult to actually try and do something, so I did the next best thing and did nothing. Even breathing was a problem because my heart was going at two hundred beats per minute and my breathing had to try and keep up with it. Holding my breath, although tempting, was not an option. After what seemed like only a small decade I began to wonder what was going to happen when the ground arrived. I started to run through some options. The best seemed to be running in mid air to help cushion the landing. I was about to put this scheme into action when the

John Clarke

ground arrived. It didn't arrive in a gentle soothing manner like a train gently pulling into a station, oh no, it arrived at about twelve hundred feet per minute of down. For those not of a metric inclination, that's about twelve miles an hour, and I say again... downwards! I ungraciously buried myself into the mud of the field. You may have seen it on the television; a climber falls, regains consciousness and starts to see if he can move his legs, arms etc.

I did it for real and yes everything was working. I crawled out from under my little red and white beauty and looked up straight into the eyes of an experienced sheep with further nearby sheep appearing to ready themselves, for applause. On second thoughts, perhaps I hit my head on landing. I don't think sheep are actually able to applaud. Nevertheless, as I sat on the ground a thought occurred to me. "I am a pilot, I have flown, I am a hang glider, I have slipped the surly bonds of earth on laughter silvered wings etc., etc... I gotta' do it again and now! Yes, yes, yes!"

The strings had broken again on the top of the glider but I was on a roll and so I dismissed this unimportant point and started to stagger back up the hill. Ever trying to learn from my mistakes I resolved to fix the rope that had caused my temporary blindness. But what with? I was in the middle of a field. I picked up a stick. This would act as a spreader bar and the rope would be either side of my ears. I have to hand it so myself, I am magnificent.

I don't know if you have walked up a six hundred foot high, steep shit laden hill with a hang glider on your back, but it's difficult, quite hard work. Some two hours later I was back at the top trying desperately to remember why I was there. Slowly my cardio-respiratory system returned to some semblance of normality. I knew I had to fly again before I bottled out,

49

Dunge Bottom

"Okay, here goes just the same as before. Except I can now see, bloody hell, oh my, oh my Goodness, get me down, get me down please!"

You see it didn't really occur to me before but I now realised I had a fear of heights and I was looking down six hundred feet (that's fifty feet higher than your average power station chimney) which in turn is a bit over half the height of Blackpool Tower. My mind tore between the two emotions of overwhelming pleasure and suffocating terror. The newly realised views were magnificent, Ilam village now glowing golden in the copper sun, the tiny white dots (sheep I presumed) running around the fields beneath me, the fresh breeze in my face, the majesty of flight! And the only thing that is stopping me from falling to my death is a thin plastic seat and two bits of rope running either side of my head. Also curing the blindness did have a knock on effect because it effectively shortened the length of the ropes and now my legs were firmly trapped under the aluminium bar in front of me. I need to explain the significance of this to you if you will indulge me for a moment.

Imagine, if you can, going on a Saga Bondage Holiday at the World of Leather Centre in Cleethorpes, one sultry week in August. Actually this could be any World of Leather and the season doesn't matter but this is my story so that's how it is. Anyway, there you are blindfolded, semi-naked and trussed up in a rather tight fitting chamois leather outfit. Your hands firmly tied behind your back and a broad leather strap fastened around your knees. You now hear from somewhere in your darkness the tip tapping of the Dominatrix's high heels on the polished wood floor, the occasional 'snap' of her whip cracking the air. Panic sets in and you try and run, except you cannot, you are hobbled,

John Clarke

you fall forwards, feeling the splinters from the floor penetrating your bare skin, the tip tapping gets louder and louder, you cannot escape, and resigned to your fate, you can only surrender. I do appreciate that we may inhabit differing worlds, but the point is, running when you are tied up is, well....tricky. Therefore as running on landing was now completely out of the question, I needed to come up with another landing strategy. After due deliberation, closing my eyes again seemed a good option and then simply wait until I hit the ground. To my relief this was a complete success! I once again unerringly found the ground and assumed the crumpled heap position with no neurological deficit or broken bones...

"I am a bird man."

"That was a crap landing." said a voice.

And that's when I met Colin....

4

Colin

"**I** beg your pardon"

I got up fully expecting to see a delegation from the Womens' Institute on a fieldtrip, but no, that was a pleasure to come. I glanced towards the voice, squinting painfully as I looked at the darkened figure, framed by the brightest of afternoon suns. I could see no detail but thought I caught a whiff of an unknown but strangely familiar scent. At this moment, he moved to one side and I could now see what lay, or rather stood, I was doing all the laying in this relationship, behind the voice. It was a Colin complete with crash helmet, a glider and a cigarillo, from which a wisp of strangely scented smoke rose up around his face, causing him to grimace against the stinging vapours. He sported a Mexican style moustache and the biggest aerodynamic nose that I have ever seen. Add this to the squint and the smoke and he reminded me of Lee Van Cleef should he ever film a gliding based Western in Derbyshire. He was about my height. His face, still twisted into a grimace, spat out a plug of what I took to be chewing tobacco. Getting back to his nose, it was the sort of nose that you simply could not stop staring at. I'm sure you know what I mean, you cannot stop staring at the wonky eye in a wonky eyed person and the same goes for noses in my book.

"Tell you what" said Colin, "if you can do another flight like that again I'll give you your certificate."

"A certificate?" I asked, hoping for an illuminatory response.

"Yep" came the staccato reply, followed by another spitting episode.

"Great, and that is?"

"A certificate" he spat back at me, fortunately without a plug of chewing tobacco this time.

I was unsure as to how I could interpret his expression and as communication was proving difficult I decided that perhaps I should just go and have another fly.

"I'll watch you from down here and if all goes well I'll sign you off. I'm the club safety officer"

"What club?" I enquired hoping against hope that I would avoid another spitting episode, as I found it somewhat unpleasant, I am but a sensitive soul. He looked at me again with that strangely unfamiliar grimace and seemed surprised that I had not heard of the Peak Hang Gliding Club, based in Derby.

I was unsure, at the time, as to whether I should question Colin on the point, but as I was still a little wary of the spitting I decided to save it for later. For the moment I couldn't believe my luck to meet another pilot and a club official to boot, the day was getting better and better.

Now how to learn from this last flight. I dared not risk

having my legs trapped under that bar again, so I need to engage my brain and come up with a fix. I was an outstanding student at school at woodwork. Well actually not that outstanding, but on the Clarke Scale of Outstandingness I was, simply because I didn't come bottom in the class. It's all relative. So putting my vast skills to good use I decided to lengthen the ropes a bit, allowing a gap between my legs and the bottom bar, therefore I would be able to run, perchance to land.

This time the ascent and subsequent recovery took three hours. Luckily Colin was a patient man and he watched intently as I did my best take off yet, about two paces in to the, now much stronger, wind.

The feeling really was mind blowing, the views this time were even better, I noticed for the first time that I was sharing the flying with some birds, puffins I believe although I was not totally sure about this as my eyes were watering. I could even hear the voices of some walkers as they glanced up to watch me, yes me, fly overhead. I could not believe that this was actually happening, it all seemed surreal. My newest problem was that I didn't seem to be coming down much. In fact I was approaching Colin in the landing field with an extra two hundred and fifty feet of height. I quickly worked out that flying like this would mean me missing the field altogether. The problem was, with the wind being stronger now at the top of the hill, there was much more lift being generated by the hill as the wind is deflected upwards. If I may explain, a glider is always sinking down through the air, due to gravity. If the wind/air, in which it is flying, is going up due to such a hill deflection at a faster rate than the glider is sinking through it then the glider will rise relative to the ground. This was exactly what happened to me, giving me that lovely extra height.

Dunge Bottom

I looked ahead and saw a wood with a pond in it, with, on the other side, a power cable, telephone lines and Ilam village.

While struggling with my dilemma I heard a faint voice from below, it was Colin, suggesting that I turn, he of course had already spotted the aforementioned hazards.

"Um, turning eh" I decided to seek clarification.

"How do I turn Colin" I called out as I sailed overhead at two hundred feet.

"Oh forget it – it's too late anyway." He replied. Somewhat less than helpful I thought, and decided to take him task about this should the next few seconds be survivable. I had not considered the eventuality of landing, that word again still used in its widest possible context, in anything other than the same field. Flight planning was not yet a concept I had heard of and certainly not one that I understood. My immediate problem was that the effects of not having a flight plan were becoming increasingly important to my current situation.

I could feel my heart pounding, my breathing matched my heart (not sure if your breaths can actually pound but it felt like it) and I had the inevitable and immediate need to poo.

My alternatives were:

Land in the trees this side of the pond.

Land in the trees on the other side of the pond.

Hit the telephone wires and power cables, generally avoided by flying folk Hit Ilam.

None of these seemed ideal. I could almost see the headlines "Dare Devil Hang Glider Pilot Crashes Into Village, Thousands Killed"

Back to the problem in hand.

"Lift my feet up to miss the trees, fly over the pond, lift

my feet up again to miss the other trees on the other side of the pond, dive under the power cables, climb over the telephone cable."

Things really were going well now. I was down to about fifty feet.

"Damn" I had taken my mind off the village. Dead ahead of me was a farmer looking out of the bedroom window of his traditional Stone built Peak Park farmhouse, complete with graded slate roof, and stone mullioned windows, red roses climbed poetically across the textured stonework. The farmer maintained eye contact with me and I thought I was going to go through the window. Suddenly the glider turned through ninety degrees to the right and I landed, in my own style, on his back lawn. I later learned from Colin that the right wing tip had hit a large tree (which I hadn't noticed) in the farmer's garden, spinning me round and forcing the landing. It must have looked impressive and completely surprising, especially to me.

"Well done lad" the farmer called out, cool as you like, "don't know why everyone doesn't do that, you're a lot nearer your car. Leave your fifty pence by the back door." The window closed and he was gone. Well what a day! Not only was I now a super hero pilot, but I had made contact with some other pilots and I had got or was going to get a certificate. Definitely time to celebrate at the nearest pub with my new found mentor.

Sitting quietly (well, not so quietly because I had consumed three pints of extra strong bitter shandy) and reliving what was a fabulous day with Colin, I start to learn one or two things about my new passion. I list them in no particular order and share them with you. The certificate I achieved is the first stage in the pilot rating system brought in by the British Hang Gliding Association. I had never even heard that there was a governing body for the sport.

This wind business, it seemed that Oomie and I had got it completely wrong. You see you need to have the wind blowing up the hill to form slope lift which can make you go up and fly higher and for longer. Apparently trying to take off with the wind blowing from behind you is almost impossible and very dangerous. What can happen with taking off downwind is that not only is the wind pushing you from behind but is also trying to tip you over as the wind gets under the back of the gliders sail, Additionally the wind is now following the slope and falling down the hill.

In those early days of hang gliding the glider's performance was very poor. By that I mean that they sank through the air (gravity again) at about eight hundred feet every minute, so if the wind is blowing down the hill at a seemingly innocent ten miles per hour which represents about one hundred feet per minute, you have to add this to the sinking speed of the glider which now means you are going down at a disconcertingly speedy nine hundred feet per minute. As Oomie and I found out, this is an uncomfortable sensation. A further issue is that it is impossible to run fast enough to get off the ground. You see a glider needs to go forwards at a minimum of fifteen miles per hour to fly, and in a no wind situation that means the pilot has to run at fifteen miles per hour to get the glider flying. So if you try and take off with the wind blowing at ten miles per hour from behind you, it follows that before moving you a have negative airspeed of ten miles per hour. Consequently you have to run at ten miles per hour initially to cancel that out. To fly now you need to run an extra fifteen miles per hour to get the speed you need. The math is simple. You have to be able to run at twenty five miles per hour while carrying a glider to take off. Mission Impossible I suspect. In summary, don't take off downwind because you have to run faster than is possible whilst falling at a suicidal rate. Well perhaps Colin does know what he is talking about because we certainly didn't take off and Oomie did almost have his spine non-surgically removed! Colin also explained the simplicity of turning the glider to me. It seems that if you want to turn left you move your weight to the left and if you want to turn right you move your weight to the right. "Pity I didn't know that before my last flight" I thought. As for the landing malarkey, well, I was told that just before you hit the ground you just push this aluminium bar out as far as it will go and you just kind of parachute down from a few feet to what would be a gentle landing, rather than descending at some twelve miles an hour. Colin also mentioned that keeping your eyes open does make things a little easier if somewhat more frightening. As he told me this I looked at him questioningly, is he being serious or sarcastic, Can I trust this man's every utterance? He was, after all, a psychiatric nurse, and so should be beyond reproach. I started to look at Colin a little more closely He was a real mine of information. "Pity I didn't manage to speak to him before we tried it out last weekend." He was the club contact that I tried to call but was in hospital.

"Not with a hang gliding injury I hope?" said I in what I hoped was a sympathetic tone.

"No" said Colin, "Piles" Bit of conversation stopper that one, except Colin then went onto mention that Norwegian for piles is hemmorides, whilst Austrian is Knottle or if you have a bunch of external thrombotic piles it is called knnottlnen, also the Spanish Royal Family have no word for piles. Did he know everything!?

Dunge Bottom

I just sat back, letting him talk as the shandy worked its soporific magic. He is going out with a radiographer called Di who works at Derby Royal Infirmary, also flies and is the club training officer. I was not sure if he was hinting at anything but he suggested that I call her and perhaps go out with her and do some training. I asked him if he really thought that I needed it now that I had obtained my certificate?

"YES! Here's her number, ring her now" was the reply, disappointing in its emphatic tone.

5

Diane

At the first opportunity I spoke to this Di woman. It was an interesting discussion, on the whole, although she sounded a bit off; going into a rant about Colin which I found difficult to fully understand. She was muttering things about him being a pest and continually demanding sex, every time they went caravanning in Harold's field in Wetton and that it wasn't very high up on her list of priorities as she was much more interested in hang gliding and photography. Which I suppose is reasonable. I eventually dragged her back to what was my priority, hopefully hang gliding again next weekend.

"I'll be at the rifle range, next Sunday at ten, do you know where it is?"

"Yes" I muttered as casually as I could, not thinking it advisable to mention my previous experiences there. "How will I recognise you?" I enquired. There was a silence at the other end of the phone. I cleared my throat "How will I recognise you?" I asked again.

"It'll be the car with the hang glider on the roof " she said, and put the phone down. I wasn't sure what sort of an impression I had just made with Di, I hoped she was kind and upportive, especially as she probably now felt she will be training some form of idiot, albeit one with a certificate!

Sunday came and I got to the rifle range an hour early. While I was waiting I became increasingly nervous. Fortunately there was a public toilet in the car park but its proximity and my nerves combined to make me increasingly dehydrated as I waited for my mentor. At least being early allowed me, between frequent disappearances into the deep dark depths of the bogs, to people watch. The area is very popular with tourists as it is handy for the local beauty spots. It would have been quite an enjoyable experience if I wasn't quite so stressed, but some tourists did certainly distract me somewhat. I was amazed by the number of ladies who turned up for a ramble or hike into the hills evidently thinking high heeled shoes were suitable footwear for such an activity. There was one particular small group of elderly hippies who turned up in a couple of VW camper vans, dressed sensibly for their planned adventure. As they walked past me I caught the unmistakable smell of wet cagoules and Ralgex. Disturbing and strangely reassuring at the same time Exactly at ten a red Ford Escort estate pulled into the car park with two hang gliders on the roof. Inside the car was a small short dark haired woman with a squint and thin mean lips. She got out of the car. I approached her, nervously clearing my throat before tripping over my untied boot laces and landing flat on my face at her feet. Not quite the first impression I had hoped to make. Dusting myself off and rising to my full height with

John Clarke

as much dignity as possible I announce my presence to Di. Now she was out of the car I noticed she was less short and on close inspection I confirmed she did have a squint that was difficult to stop staring at, "Oh no, not another defect" I thought, as well as the thinnest lips that I have ever seen. Surely I won't be able to stop staring at this woman's face. Her initial greeting surprised me:

"Hi, I'm Di, if you don't do exactly as I say you will break your arms here and here!"

"I'm sorry" I spluttered and she kindly pointed out exactly where I would break my arms, which I found informative if not totally reassuring.

We'll take the club training glider up to the hill she said, and started to walk off towards the site.

"What about the glider I called out?"

"You'll be okay, it's not very heavy..."

During the rigging of this glider, which I noted was in a calming black colour and with no spare bits left over. Diane kindly pointed out and named the different parts. At every stage she never failed to mention what would befall the pilot if each particular element should fail in flight. Generally nothing good was the overall tone. She then kindly asked me to carry the glider up the hill (fortunately the same one as Oomie and I had tried to fly off the other week, so I knew the way up to the top. This was so she could do a demo and test the conditions. Did she mean the thickness of the air or what?

Once we had reached the top of the hill Diane clipped into the glider with impressive speed. She ran a few steps and took off flying straight and true before landing perfectly on her feet next to a courting couple who remained blissfully unaware of her presence. I decided I might have to listen to this Di, as she does seem able to do it and the flight did look so smooth and easy. I dashed down to the bottom of the hill as I wanted to get into her good books somehow or other and I might, in extremis, offer to help her carry the glider back up the hill...or not... as it is a very steep hill after all.

"Bugger me, that was rough" she said when we met up at the bottom.

"Really?" I retorted, wondering what aspect of the flight she was referring to, the harness, a thistle injury in a finger perhaps. At this point my mind started wandering off. I was soon brought back to earth by Di saying that there was no chance for me flying until it calmed down a bit. I plucked up the courage to ask Di what she was talking about. She said something along the lines that the wind was too strong and the hill immediately in front of us (our very own Table Top Mountain you will recall) was causing the air to be very turbulent and unpredictable and this often happened at this training hill. I later learned that wind or air likes to flow along in an uninterrupted manner. So if you stick an obstacle up in the airflow then of course the air has to go around it. Sometimes it can do this in a smooth way without disturbing itself too much but other times it will cause the air to swirl around and be very variable and gusty. Naturally putting up a five hundred foot high hill would certainly affect this smooth flow and make things pretty rough.

"What do we do then?" I asked

"Wait" was the reply.

I had begun to notice that conversation wasn't really flowing between Di and myself. Usually when I'm nervous I can't stop talking or going to the toilet.

"What's it like then?" said a tiny voice from behind me. I looked over my shoulder and saw an equally tiny man, with a huge black compensatory beard. His name was Richard

John Clarke

and he was carrying a tiny glider over his shoulder followed by a tiny young lady, minus a beard.

"Crap" was Di's reply. "Really bumpy"

I must try and remember some of these technical terms for later use.

"I'll rig anyway" said the tiny voice.

Di then tried to point out the differences between the tiny glider which was an advanced Skyhook model and the training one. To me the differences were obvious, firstly it wasn't all black, in fact it was mostly white, it was also tiny, and the sail was much flatter and less baggy than the one we were flying. Di explained to me that a tight sail was much more efficient than a baggy one and so improved performance quite a lot.

I must admit that tiny Richard was most impressive as he had an all white one piece flying suit and helmet and really did match his tiny glider. He walked up to the top of the hill much faster than I expected because of the tiny legs. Once at the top he turned round and took off without hesitation, flew over our heads in silence, presumably because of the tightness of his sail, waved and casually called out that it was indeed "crap and really bumpy" before he turned left and disappeared in the direction of the cars, with his tiny girl friend following on behind. I felt a little sorry for her as she had to carry all the bags and other paraphernalia involved in hang gliding back to the car park. Didn't seem much of a deal for her, still love is blind I suppose.

"Bloody hell" I thought "that was dead impressive."

"He hates walking" said Di, "He always tries to land back near the car park"

I thought it might be an idea to casually mention to her that I actually did have a glider and had flown off Bunster Hill three times last weekend.

Dunge Bottom

"The hell you have "said Di "what are we doing here then?"

"Because you said so." I mentioned nervously.

"Bollocks! We'll go over to Bunster now. The wind will be okay there I think. And stop pratting about here.

"Di really does know her stuff " I thought to myself as we arrived at Bunster Hill. She had shown me a road which wound its way up to the top. My legs had still not recovered from the three ascents up the main north of face of the behemoth that they had undertaken last weekend!!

"You carry the club glider and I'll bring my own" she said leading off into the distance towards the summit.

Only mildly exhausted this time I gazed down at the almost vertical face , the green landing fields far below, still dotted with sheep and the village still way off in the distance.

"Tell me what happened last time you flew here" she demanded.

I tried to tell her leaving out the most embarrassing bits. She smiled thinly and looked quizzically at me seemingly slightly impressed. If there was a 'slightly impressed' scale, say, one to ten, I think I was a solid two. I did feel, in view of my last flight, that I really should talk about turning, getting confirmation of the instructions Colin gave me last week end, after all I mightnot be able to rely on the same tree to assist my landing this time. I asked the question.

"Easy" answered Di. Move left to go left, move right to go right, pull the bar in to go faster, push out the bar to slow down.

"That sounds easy. Is it easier if you keep your eyes open?" I tried to sound casual. For the first time Di smiled, looked at me strangely, and then laughed. I decided to keep my mouth shut.

John Clarke

A wise decision as it turned out. For it seemed that I had unwittingly passed some form of test from Di and was now accepted. She was now my new mentor.

"I'll go first" she said. "And show you the best landing area" Mind you Di did seem to take an enormous amount of time rigging her glider and then checking it, (she did this several times). I was not too sure how confident Di actually was but eventually she muttered:

"Better get the show on the road" What is it with hang gliding and American movies? With that she picked up her glider and disappeared into the wild blue yonder.

She seemed to fly miles out away from the face of the hill and after a few turns she once again landed perfectly in the middle of the green field with the white dots in it. It looked really impressive but the whole thing probably took less than a minute. I could not help but wonder about the cost benefit equation. You could take about an hour to carry up the glider up the hill and then have a flight lasting one minute. Still it did look amazing.

"Right Clarkey here we go, I'll just follow her flight path and all will be well." I marvelled at my confidence.

Take-off was easy. I still couldn't seem to keep my feet on the ground as it does simply disappear from under your feet!

"Okay, time for one of those turns, now what did she say? turn left move left, easy …. Ok here goes. I moved my body to the left and wait. Nothing happens, move further over… still nothing happens, I've now moved all the way over and…suddenly the glider turned left, Oh the relief!"

I noticed that Di was behind me and the hill I just took off from was approaching at high speed. "This could be a problem" I thought. I tried moving right and slowly the glider turned a little to the right and levelled off.

Dunge Bottom

"Phew, what a relief." Things seemed to be developing quite quickly. I was aware that the village had disappeared as had Di, the landing field and the sheep. Bunster Hill was now on my left and approaching very quickly and I also saw for the first time that there is a lower ridge which joins onto the main hill immediately in front of me, fortunately the ridge was below me and I thought I would clear it quite easily. In the distance I saw my old favourite flat topped hill. A great relief as at least I was flying towards, familiar territory, so I shouldn't get lost.

"Where to land though?" I wondered. Not too keen on this turning business however, I think I'll just keep flying in a straight line at least there are a few big fields in front of me."

And a small tree.

I noticed over the remaining time of the flight that the small tree was increasingly less small, and as I got close to it, it assumed the proportions of a large bushy tree. Whilst trying to work out how to avoid the tree I hit it. It must have been most amusing to the group of medieval re-enactment society members out for their Sunday ramble to see this sky God hit a tree and literally bounce backwards out of it landing on his arse, this time, quite gently and with no damage. A large round of applause greets me as I shakily stand up and dust myself off.

"You'll get a badge for that" laughs a voice from nearby!

I look around, preparing to reply with vicious sarcasm and innuendo, when I see the voice. He has a genuine smile on his face and a glider on his shoulder and declares that his name is Roger. Oddly enough Roger also has a dodgy looking moustache, a little like Colin's, but reassuringly a non aerodynamic nose, which is a great relief I can tell you.

He is about six feet tall with brown hair and extremely

John Clarke

large hands and feet judging by the size of his boots, that's his feet of course not his hands. In fact they are so big it's becoming increasingly difficult not to stare fixedly at them. Bloody hell he has just smiled, the size of his teeth beggars belief and so white. Is it me? Help me someone please! What is wrong with these people?... Hang glider pilots are starting to seem to be like caricatures out of the League of Gentlemen.

"Just saw your flight off the top. No one has done that before, you must have been flying a lot to come down wind behind the hill like that and survive. Pity about the tree though".

I was about to say "Are you taking the piss?" but then I looked at him again, and thought that perhaps he wasn't. Roger turns out to be the hang gliding club secretary. I'm meeting them all now.

"I'll help you back to the car park" he says and leads me off in reverse back towards the ridge and the village. We arrived at the bottom car park at the same time as Di. I smiled at her, then frowned at her and then felt like running away. Her face looked like thunder, her lips now totally disappeared and the squint, oh God the squint. I was beginning to realise that when she was angry her squint became more pronounced. It was now almost impossible to look at both of her eyes without either swivelling one's head rapidly from side to side with the obvious risk of a whiplash type injury or keeping the head still and doing the swivelling with the eyeballs, with the attendant risk of causing a seizure. I guessed she is not best pleased for some reason.

"What the hell were you playing at!!!" she spat out.

"Well." was all I was allowed to say. I will spare you, dear reader, from the vitriolic invective which heaped itself upon

69

Dunge Bottom

me from the lipless mouth.

Later I realized that Di was really concerned that I had gone out and killed myself, as she last saw me disappearing downwind at high speed over the hill. I might need some more practice yet.

I decided to take Roger for a drink, he seemed a little more friendly and approachable than Di who, at the moment, was flatly refusing to go with us, declaring that she needed to go off and cool down before she hit me

We went on to Ye Olde Royal Oake at Wetton, apparently a favourite for the hang gliding club members. They even had a camping barn in the village. I'd not been there before and it seemed a typical Peak District country pub, white washed limestone walls, with a blue tiled roof, inside were a couple of rooms with stone flagged floors placed either side of the semi circular bar. One of the rooms had a roaring log fire and it was to this that we naturally gravitated. Roger seemed to be full of info' and was very encouraging, in fact he invited me to join the local club based in Derby and come along to the next club meeting which was every Wednesday at the Mitre Hotel in Derby. This was a major breakthrough on my upwards, and occasionally downward, learning curve. This was too good to be true so I got the directions and promised to see him there.

Wednesday night came and I was feeling ill at ease, I'm not always relaxed walking into an unfamiliar city pub alone. You never quite know who might frequent such a place, however, on sticking my head around the door it did appear to be reasonably safe looking with a smiling landlord. I ventured bravely in and ordered a bitter shandy casually looking around the smoke filled room trying to spot any likely looking hang glider experts.

What would they look like? Slicked back hair, obvious

six packs, Rayban shades, piercing eyes and a sneering mouth, all about six foot six tall. Well I didn't look like that, but then I wasn't an expert was I?

The pub was a typical town sort of pub, ever so slightly faded with a hint of jaded thrown in for good measure. The bar was relatively empty with just one or two likely suspects, mind you one of them has just slid down the front of the bar and collapsed unconscious onto the compulsory sticky carpet, fortunately already in the recovery position so my Scouting first aid experience was not called for. I noticed the landlord ignored this and just made a quick phone call and I found out later that this is a regular activity of this "local". Oddly enough, a couple walked through the door, with a limb in plaster each accompanied by two paramedics. I wondered if they were chasing new NHS targets and cheating by bringing their own patients along with them. But no, the cripples disappeared into the back room whilst the paramedics help the collapsed man. Strangely they seemed to know his name and dragged him off into the ambulance waiting outside.

I turned back to the bar and noticed a bloke of about thirty years of age. He had a loud voice which would no doubt carry far on the wind. He was also on crutches. He ordered a drink and was joined by someone with an arm in plaster. I wondered whether this was a violent neighbourhood and my thoughts turned to trying to get home in one piece. Not completely sure my initial risk assessment of this establishment was correct, I watched the two men furtively, they looked like tough sorts.

"Hi Ron, how's the leg going on?" said the newcomer.

"About as good as your arm, Eric" he sarcastically returned. Both of them chuckled gently at their witty repartee.

Dunge Bottom

"I've only just started driving again" continued Ron, "it's the first club night I've been to since the crash." I wondered if he was referring to some road traffic collision, a motor bike perhaps? I continued my musings until I thought that I heard them refer to Roger, Di and a Colin! It seemed a bit of a coincidence this, as I had only just made acquaintance of a Roger, Di and Colin myself. I was getting a bit worried now because time was getting on and I could not pick out any obvious hang gliding types at all. However I was rescued by my Roger walking through the door. He called out a greeting to the barman, and the two cripples at the bar and turns beaming towards me, bloody hell those teeth...

"You made it then" he said. "Sorry I'm a bit late but I needed to finish some embroidery first"

"Embroidery" I knew there was more to this bloke that at first appeared. Worryingly so, as well.

"Come on through and meet the gang" says Roger, leading me through into the back. He showed me to a dimly lit, smoke filled room, with sticky carpets, continuing the theme, a gentle scent of antiseptic and old socks. At least I hoped it was old socks. It was filled with thirty to forty people of which a good third had something or other in Plaster of Paris. So this was where the club meeting was held! The quantity of plaster was a bit off putting though.

I sat quietly in a corner, eavesdropping on some conversations. I assumed that they were using the English language but they did not appear to be making any sense as there was a plethora of very strange sounding words and phrases being used like; washout, washin, dihedral, snotty, bumpy, rotor, etc the list went on and on.

"What strange world am I in?" thought I. At that point Roger stood up and called the meeting to order. I quietly followed the discussions as best as I could. There was much talk of new site restrictions due to the forthcoming lambing (I was seriously wondering what sort of perverts I've glimpsed in this under-world masquerading as a hang gliding club. I considered trying to make my escape when the spotlight suddenly fell on me.

"I'd like to welcome a new member" called out Roger looking and pointing at me, "Meet John." Everyone stopped and looked at me in an eerie silence, so deep you could hear a crutch fall onto a sticky carpet. In actual fact a crutch did fall onto the sticky carpet as Ron, who had both legs in plaster and had enjoyed a number of dry white wines since I last saw him, fell to the floor with a gentle grin on his face. I smiled in what I hoped was a friendly way, but with my palsy you could never tell. I stood up, gave a little wave and sat down again. Then I stood up again as Roger said he would like to present me with my first club badge.

"What the hell is he talking about?" I thought as I looked towards the exit and noticed that it was covered by Di.

"Bugger no escape there."

Roger went on to tell about my tree landing exploits much to the amusement of all. Then he called me forward to accept the Tree landing badge that he had only just finished embroidering himself that night. I stepped in front of the assembled masses and shook hands. As I accepted the badge I noted that my hand was completely engulfed in his, Hell, his hands were enormous, and in an effort to avoid looking at his teeth I casually glanced downwards and there were his gargantuan feet. Although it was embarrassing it did reassure me about Roger and his embroidery. I had not up to this point in my life come across many men who embroider and are into lambing. Although of course with my politically correct hat on, I must declare that a man enjoying both embroidery and lambing is not per se wrong, unless of course lambing constitutes a criminal offence similar to muffin the mule. Colin then stood up and awarded me my certificate to loud applause from some of the assembled throng. Some however were unable to clap as their clapping equipment was encased in plaster. I was now to be classed as a qualified hang gliding pilot, what a meteoric rise to fame. Even I was impressed. People whom I had never met were keen to congratulate me, which was kind. They were a friendly bunch, although I was reluctant to discuss the "lambing issue" immediately. I saw tiny Richard again along with his tiny wife, and I did my best to make my peace with Di who magnanimously pointed out that I am on my own now, but she always carries inflatable splints in her car as she is also the clubs first aid officer as well as the training bod. The two areas did seem to go hand in hand.

Over the course of the evening I was offered drinks and tips on the best sites to fly and would I like to buddy up with anyone, who can show me around the dozen or so flying sites that are controlled by the club? It actually turned out to be a very jolly event and through the foggy haze of those extra bitter shandies, I begin to feel comfortable in this strange new world.

In fact it was the start of something that was to turn into a full time occupation and dominate my life for the next twenty six years. One day I would reach the giddy heights of Hang Gliding Instructor. But for now, well that's a long, long way off.

A Beard You Could Hide a Badger In...

Over the next year or so I did as much hang gliding as I could and started to make many new friends who, like me, were always hoping to fly higher and further and be able to soar more easily. To that end we were always on the lookout

John Clarke

for better performing gliders so it seemed that fate played a hand when Malcolm, you will remember smoked a pipe and had an enormous beard as well as a hang gliding school in Brighton, telephoned me out of the blue to tell me he was now the UK importer for an American high performance glider. He was keen to come up to the Peak District and demonstrate it to our flying club in the hope of a few orders.

"I suppose you are still flying those rag bag gliders up there?" he said sarcastically. "Still doing top to bottoms?"

"No" I replied, stung by his jibe. "We don't just fly top to bottom. One of our members flew and landed back on top of Bunster Hill last month. He gave a whistle of, what I took to be admiration. I had omitted to say that this occurrence was due to the wind becoming very strong and the unfortunate pilot was blown backwards over the top of the hill only to have his flight arrested by a line of tall trees. At the last bulletin it was pronounced that he was doing well and would be out of hospital in a couple of weeks.

The sneering continued.

"Well if you flew our Wills Wings Super Swallowtails, you'd be top landing all the time. How about me and my team come up and show you lot how it's done?"

So it was in the blazing hot summer of 1976 that I arranged for him and his "team" to come up and meet with as many club members as possible to show us his super wings and I suppose his super skills. The selected site was Bunster Hill and the assembled masses duly arrived to bear witness to the super events to come. Actually there were about ten club members and The Brighton Team. They were due to fly the side of Bunster Hill where a young pilot had an earlier brush with a lone tree. It was very hot and the top of the hill was covered in waist high thistles. I must admit that we were all a bit excited by the sight of the new gliders and the test pilots. The gliders they were demonstrating certainly did look very different from ours, they were much bigger and wider than our old rag bags and the sails apart from being all white were much tauter. As for the test pilots, well they looked seriously cool with your actual Raybans, smart blue all in one fitted flying suits, and large sparkly crash helmets. They certainly put me and my fellow club members, in the shade somewhat with our olive coloured Gamages anoraks and pudding basin headgear. Perhaps these guys flying these gliders really would impress. The air of excitement and expectation grew. Anyway the super heroes start to ask questions like…

"How high is the airspace above this hill?"

The general response, from the assembled club fliers, was "what the bloody hell are they talking about?" I mean all we have ever done here is take off and fly down to the gently sloping field in the bottom and land!

"What's the club XC record from here, and any airspace restrictions downwind"? Following our blank look we were informed that XC referred to Cross Country record, i.e., the furthest distance anyone has flown from the hill and airspace restrictions meant the airspace where the big silver birds in the sky live, best avoided and ever so slightly illegal for hang gliders as we didn't have the required instrumentation or indeed oxygen. Once again mutterings were heard from the club members:

"Taking the piss,"

"What are they on?"

"Anyone smell wacky baccy?"

"I'm awfully sorry but I have no idea what you are talking about" This last muttering came from Ron one of our club fliers. He tried to be helpful.

"If you are desperate you might just make it over the top

of the hill and land near Polly's shop in Milldale.

"Really?" replied the bearded one

"Yes, but my concern is there's nowhere to land, you see. If you try to land in the river you might upset the ducks, we have several of the less common breeds and they are an important part of the ecosystem of the dale. The ecosystem itself is…" It was here that several other club members dragged him off in mid sentence, as Ron had a reputation for talking at great lengths on such matters, with the attendant risk of people leaping off the hill regardless of whether they were attached to a glider or not.

"What's the bottom landing like?" Tony, one of the bearded one's cohorts, asked warily

"You can land in the enormous green field at the bottom of the hill, no problems" I told him, being keen to impress. I also added, knowingly, that the tree on the left boundary hedge could be a problem and pilots should exercise great care when anywhere near it! Not naming any names of course.

After a pipe or two of baccy, Malcolm (to be brutally honest I could not take the title of super hero seriously when he turns out to be called Malcolm) and cronies rigged their gliders and asked for help to launch them. They wanted someone to help by holding the front wires of the glider to steady it before they ran off the hill into the wild blue yonder. I was one of the keen ones and eager to show the rest of the club that I had a natural affinity with these super slick flyers from 'down south' and so I volunteered to hold Malcolm's nose. I know, I know. This is probably conjuring up the weirdest picture in your mind. It meant that I would be holding the front wires of the glider referred to earlier. Malcolm spent some time looking forward and up into the clear blue sky and muttering about thermals, thistle devils, swallows coming close and other pagan type utterances. Upon hearing such utterances the assembled club members were getting bored and restless and there were more mutterings of

"What the hell is he talking about now?"

Suddenly Malcolm stood up and called out, to no one in particular.

"See you at cloud base"

One of his Raybanned cohorts loudly called out "We'll be right behind you."

At this point Malcolm counted one, two, three and charged down the hill at warp speed. I have to admit that this did cause me some confusion. Firstly the cry about cloud base seemed optimistic as there were no clouds at all but worst of all was what the hell did mean by one, two three? I was about to find out. I was standing directly in front of Malcolm when he started to count and was in the process of working through the meaning of this counting when he charged at full speed straight towards me. Now he was a large chap and carried a great deal of momentum. I was initially confused by his exasperated cry of:

"Get out of the sodding way!" just as he ran over me.

It then of course became much less confusing as I now knew what one two three meant. Presumably he was expecting me to move out of the way just prior to the count of three. Oh well next time.

I was lying flat on my back in the deepest sharpest thistles available on Bunster Hill. From my new vantage point I dozily admired the still clear blue azure sky and noted that there was no sign of Malcolm and his all white Super Swallowtail. I struggled painfully to my feet, looked up and all around expecting to see him climbing higher and higher to the blue vault above. There was another loud cry of one, two, three, whereupon I immediately dived to the ground again in the interests of self preservation. I forgot the thistles. I was now covered in thistle barbs, front and back. For those of you perhaps mainly urban dwellers who have little knowledge of the world of thistles, then this was a particularly painful incident and would take until Christmas to finally remove all of the bloody things from my tortured punctured and lacerated skin..

The count had come from Malcolm's two chums who decided to take off almost immediately after him. Anyway I continued gazing skywards trying desperately to see these sky Gods climbing away into the heavens, but no they were not to be seen.

"They'll hit those bloody trees if there not careful" someone close by muttered.

This gave me the clue that perhaps I should be looking downwards towards the landing field? Sure enough the three super stars had descended rapidly towards the large landing field and seemed to be very close to the ground. You might remember that earlier I mentioned that we landed at the bottom in a gently sloping field. This was no problem with our very low performing hang gliders, but the heroes were flying higher performance gliders which glided down at the same angle as the field. This had the effect for them not landing at all since the ground just wasn't getting any closer. I was relieved to see that they had heeded my advice about not going anywhere near the tree to the left that I had a personal relationship with, but had chosen to fly down the field.

"Sensible chaps" I thought. The edge of the field they were flying towards was bounded by a line of large trees with just one gap slightly off centre. Beyond the trees was the road from Ilam to Thorpe and beyond that the river with large friendly looking fields beyond. I could feel their concern as the three of them rapidly approached the line of trees.

"What to do eh, what to do?" someone from our crowd muttered. This comment galvanized the other club members in to a debate.

"They hadn't better hit those trees, they'll have to turn round and land up hill and downwind,"

"Don't be daft, they should try and fly through the gap"

"It's not big enough they'll just catch the branches and land in the river"

"Bloody hell they'll drown"

The suggestions stopped abruptly as two of the flyers decided to use the trees very much as I had done previously and flew straight into them before bouncing out backwards to land unceremoniously on their arses. The third perhaps being more adventurous decided to go for the gap between the trees, fly over the road, swoop over the river and land in the fields beyond. Brilliant plan I must admit, and from our viewpoint some quarter of a mile away seemed perfectly reasonable.

Shame it didn't work.

He cleared the trees okay, skimmed over the roof of a passing car and landed slap bang in the river. Fortunately it wasn't too deep, although fast flowing. He lost his balance and was being swept downstream in quite an undignified manner when a barbed wire fence running across the river stopped him.

"Lucky bugger" someone commented.

"I'm bloody glad I didn't tell them that the big field was okay to land in" muttered Ron. "That's three gliders written off, let alone any personal injury. They're going to be hopping mad, that is if they can actually hop after what's

John Clarke

happened to them!"

At that moment, thin lips Di very kindly reminded me that it was I who had talked to them about the landing area. I couldn't help but see a glint of mischief in one of her eyes, the one without the squint, the squinty one being incapable of glinting. I admit to cowardice here and left the scene of devastation at high speed. However, Malcolm did get his revenge, because some years later I went to work for him as an instructor and hang glider builder when he relocated his hang gliding business to the Peak District.

On looking back I realize I was in at the halcyon days of hang gliding. There were no real regulations, people would just see a picture of a hang glider in a magazine and nip into their garage and make a foot-launched flying machine. I know it's hard to believe but I remember being asked at the top of Bunster Hill, one gentle day in July, if I would like to try out this new glider. I was enthusiastic on voicing my agreement, but rather regretting my utterance when I noticed that it was completely made out of plastic rainwater piping, plastic sheeting for the sail and all held together with sticky tape. I admit that I thought Peter, one of our new club members was joking at first but looking deeply into his eyes I realised he wasn't.

"You see I saw the plans for it in Home and Garden and had some spare bits left over from reroofing my garage so I thought I'd have ago" he said by way of explanation. It was dead easy to make and at least it's very light to carry up hills," he continued.

Having said yes, I was finding it increasingly difficult to come up with a reason to say no. I considered faking an epileptic fit but thought better of it. I must say on picking it up that it really was very light indeed and extremely floppy. I was not too reassured to note that the plastic sheeting was coming loose from the thin plastic wing tubing as the sticky tape needed smoothing back on again.

"Did Homes and Gardens have a flight test report about this" I enquired with a hint of fear and desperation, still looking for a way out.

"Not as such but the editor did comment how good it should be being such light weight and so easy to repair should there be any mishaps."

"So they didn't actually fly it then?"

"No but the designer was quoted as saying that turning will be a dream because of the flexibility of the wing tubes" he further continued in what I suspect he thought was an encouraging tone.

I had now run out of escape routes, I am going to have to fly it. So I flew it down Bunster Hill and I can only say that in flight all the plastic tubes assumed the shape of a huge letter S and the ripping sound of the sail slowly departing from the sticky tape, was an added distraction. Because of the now new shape of the flying machine, being ultra flexible, its performance was appalling and it only just made the very bottom of the hill. Pete, the builder of this wondrous contraption, quickly arrived asking excitedly,

"How did it go? "

I sarcastically muttered something about probably being a bit too heavy for it since I seemed to sink down very quickly.

"What was the performance like when you flew it?" I naively asked.

"Don't know" came the excited response, "It's never been flown before."

There was another guy Alan, who was a mushroom specialist. He thought that by building a glider as big as possible then he would be able to fly higher and further than anyone else. He ended up building an all black glider, made out of aluminium tubing and rip stop nylon for the sail, none of this plastic rubbish for him. We later found out, by someone tripping over a glider and actually falling through a sail, that it was made of the same rip stop nylon which weakened dramatically under ultra violet light, namely sunshine. Alan's glider ended up being three hundred square feet in size, (over double the size of a normal hang glider) In fact when he flew it the earth went dark and a great shadow was cast upon our land. His expectations for his enormous glider were spoiled a little, as he wasn't heavy enough to turn it or if the wind rose above about twelve miles per hour, he just reversed into the nearest hill The problem was that to turn the glider he had to move his weight sideways and as this was such a big glider Alan hadn't enough physical weight to have any effect on it at all, so it just carried on in a straight line. The same with flying forwards. Normally you pull your body weight towards the front of the glider which tilts the front down making it dive and go forwards and faster, unless the wind gets too strong and you go backwards. So reluctantly he reverted back to the more normal size of hang gliders.

As I mentioned earlier, I do feel very privileged to have been around in those very early pioneering years of hang gliding. So many of our drug crazed days were spent lying on sunlit hilltops, waiting for the wind to pick up/slow down/change direction etc., basking in the camaraderie of true pioneers, although we didn't really realise this at the time. We were driven by the intoxicating effects of Fishermans Friends and Night Nurse, harder substances having not really penetrated the Peaks. We still referred to a trip to Longnor (Pop. 37) as 'going into town'. Every day was an adventure; new skills were being learnt all the time.

Dunge Bottom

People seeing a hang glider on the car roof would stop to ask what is was and upon finding out be fascinated. We were considered as being daredevils, mad, crazy, heroes and bloody idiots all at the same time. You would see news paper headlines typically following crashes which were plentiful, "BIRDMAN OF DOVEDALE PLUNGES 500" FEET AND LIVES".

Being totally committed to my new hobby and having done a considerable amount of hang gliding I realised that I seemed to be doing an awful lot of walking up hills for generally a bit of a fly down. As I still found walking upwards hard work I decided it would be nice to have more time in the air with less actual physical activity. If only there was a way of getting up a hill more easily, in fact a bit like they do when skiing, on a chair lift. One day when I was pondering this I remembered reading the Readers' Digest Book of Early Aviation. A strange sounding name popped up, now what was it?... Oh yes.

Mr. Otto Lillienthal, I told you it was a strange name but he was foreign after all. His story goes something like...............Lillienthal was a German who lived in the 1800s, oddly enough in Germany. After watching birds fly and reading the musings of Leonardo da Vinci he decided that it should be possible for man to fly also. He realized that the internal combustion engine had not been invented so he was resigned to developing a foot launched glider. He built this out of wood and fabric and spent many unsuccessful hours running around the flat fields of his native countryside, ricocheting off hedges etc., without actually leaving the ground.

Eventually Otto realized that his glider needed to be on some form of hill or mountain to make it have any chance of working at all.

John Clarke

Now at this point I should mention that the part of Germany in which he lived was completely flat with obvious disadvantages for gliding. I suspect that most normal people would have perhaps moved the entire operation to, say, Bavaria, where there are plenty of hills and mountains. But not so Otto, he was made of sterner stuff and rose to the challenge by building his own hill! How cool is that? He also worked out that it would need to vaguely circular to cope with differing wind directions and additionally, getting his glider up to the top would be made much easier if there was some form of ski lift arrangement. Of course this proved initially tricky as downhill skiing had yet to be invented, so the idea of a lift was yet another area crying out for development. Incidentally, it is oft said that not only was he the father of hang gliding but also the whole of the German skiing industry.

Anyhow back to the hang gliding business.......

Initially he started at the bottom of his hill with little hops down whilst suspended by his arm pits, steering by swinging his legs around. Over a period of some years he continued to develop his hang gliders, slowly refining them to make them more stable, better performing and easier to steer. In fact he made approximately two thousand flights altogether before excessively sweaty armpits caused him to slip and fall to his death...........Bugger!! So like a blinding flash it came to me. Follow in Ottos footsteps, build a circular hill with a ski lift...Brilliant. I immediately contacted the Peak Park Planning Authority who I must admit were slightly less encouraging than I would I have liked. Actually they were entirely negative in fact their response to my entirely reasonable request was "never in a month of bloody Sundays" followed by roars of corporate laughter which

Dunge Bottom

echoed throughout the poster strewn walls of the Planning Dept.

Bastards.

I needed to think of another way of flying with reduced physical effort, "now what could that be?" I wondered....

6

Then There Was A Microlight...

It all started with a telephone call from, can you believe the name, Len Gabriels of Skyhooks, Oldham, Ltd. Manufacturers of hang gliders. I first met Len awhile back when I was selling hang gliders and as he made some of the best it was natural to deal with him. When ever I got an invite to meet up with Len I accepted with alacrity, for I found out that he was a real inventor and always came up with interesting ideas. At the time he was in his mid to late forties and working out of a mill in Oldham where his company was based. He had started out designing a machine for rolling wall paper which eventually sold all over the world before Len graduated to making things more aerodynamic. He was also heavily into radio controlled model flying so it was natural for him to get into hang gliding and more.

"Can I come and test fly something on your airfield?" he he asked. Now this did take me a little by surprise as I cannot remember actually owning an airfield. He might

Dunge Bottom

mean the disused one at Ashbourne from which I did do some tow-launched hang gliding.

"Of course no problem" I replied. This sounded intriguing

"Right see you there tonight at exactly six o'clock, come alone!" he said he before ringing off. I admit I was curious as I had seen some of Len's prototypes before. With one particular design he had stuck a small wing at the front of the main sail and it looked as if it was flying backwards. It didn't work all that well, some of them didn't, but an awful lot of his designs were brilliant and ahead of their times.. What they all had in common was that they did need hills and things to fly from. The airfield in Ashbourne was not hilly at all.

I arrived promptly at six o clock as per Len's orders. Equally promptly, at six thirty, Len and his Volvo estate arrived at the airfield. The light was just beginning to fall as he screeched to a stop and there was a very gentle westerly breeze ruffling the fallen leaves that scattered the rough broken concrete surface. He leapt out of the car, looked around furtively and whispered.

"There's no press about is there?"

"I don't think so," said I, "Do you want some, because I can always call someone from the local paper, although I'm not sure that they could come out at this short notice?" I rambled.

"No press" he whispered, "this is top secret." We were in the middle of an airfield with a thousand yards of open ground on all sides...and he was whispering, what could this be?

"Start rigging the glider for me will you?" he muttered whilst continuing to look round nervously.

"Right oh," I said thinking, lazy bugger can't he rig his own glider. I should have known that something else was

88

at the back or indeed the front of his mind. For he started to unload a lot of tubing, wheels, propeller, engine and a deck chair from the back of the car. I was too busy to take much notice as the light was beginning to fall even faster now and Len was obviously in a hurry to complete his mission, whatever that was.

After about half an hour he had assembled a deckchair on wheels with an engine and propeller at the back. In front of the engine was a construction of aluminium tubing which formed a sort of triangle above with a metal bracket at the top and an enormous nut and bolt holding it all together.

"What's that then?" I asked in all innocence.

"A powered hang glider obviously" he said looking at me as if I was taking the piss.

"Of course it is" I thought.

He was very keen to attach it to the glider I had rigged for him before anyone spotted it. He put on the necessary safety gear, a pair of gloves, pulled a cord on the engine which made the engine splutter into life, sat in the deckchair, made the engine rev louder somehow and sped off down the tarmac of the old runway. After a remarkably short distance it took off ! He gently climbed to about a thousand feet, flew round the airfield a couple of times, then lined up with the runway and landed where he took off from.

"Bloody Brilliant;" I was enthralled.

"Len that was fantastic" I said running up to him, then running away again as the propeller was still whizzing around at the back. He stopped the engine and coincidentally the propeller stopped at the same time.

"How many times have you flown it" I said, still in awe of Len.

"First flight ever" he grinned back at me.

"Want a go?" he invited

Dunge Bottom

"You bet!" was my instant response. I could just imagine sitting comfortably in the deck chair, whilst gently climbing up into the wild blue yonder, although by now it would be fairer to describe it as the wild very nearly dark yonder. I pictured casually looking down on the darkening airfield and seeing the glow of the street lights firing up over Ashbourne, all without physical effort.

"How do you fly it then?" I asked expecting a detailed instructional package of lectures, presentations and examinations prior to my tyro flight in this amazing contraption. He responded equipment... the gloves. Starting the engine he shouted:

"Pull this bicycle brake lever to rev the engine to maximum, steer it straight down the runway and after you have taken off fly round a bit and when you want to land aim at the runway and let go of the bicycle brake lever and land."

"Oh" I was about to ask for a little more clarification, when he shouted something about hurrying up as there wasn't much petrol left in it and it was very nearly dark. He then scurried away.

"Oh dear now what did he say again?" I said to myself as I was confronted by the aluminium triangle of the hang glider's control frame on which was attached the said bicycle brake lever where the cable went up to the throttle on the engine. My feet were stuck out straight in front of me and were resting on a metal bar that ran side to side and which in turn was attached to the front wheel. Pull the bicycle brake lever. "Bloody hell" I gasped as this deckchair started to accelerate quickly down the runway accompanied by an ear piercing, screeching noise from the engine, positioned just behind my head. As the machine accelerated there were bits of grit and leaves being picked up by the front wheel and blown back into my eyes, which was somewhat distracting. Fortunately my path down the runway was arrow straight and seemingly without effort the machine took off and the ground just dropped away beneath me.

It was magical for no longer was I being bombarded by leaves and grit, but I was climbing away quite rapidly whilst still being accompanied by the screeching noise from the engine. I was exhilarated and pooping myself, all at the same time and needed to work on my breathing rate to try and bring it back under control.

"Shit what did he say next", I said out loud. Then I remembered. After takeoff I was to fly around a bit. To my surprise the glider turned left and right, the same as a hang glider. After what seemed a very short space of time I appeared to be a lot higher than I expected and it also appeared to be getting much darker on the ground as well. Len later told me that it looked as if he had reached about a thousand feet above the airfield and that it looked dead impressive. From that lofty position I looked down and saw tendrils of mist were slowly working their way along the valley bottoms, illuminated by the glow of the setting sun. A beautiful sight indeed.

It really was getting very dark down below now and I had difficulty in making out Len's Volvo so landing seemed to be the best option. I desperately tried to remember what Len had told me, something to do with the bicycle brake lever? I decided to apply logic to the situation. I was gripping the bicycle brake lever with a strength that made the phrase 'death grip' seem like a gentle caress. My fingers were bent in a claw and were rapidly losing feeling. I have often found that squeezing bits of aircraft very hard is a normal reaction for me when flying and being stressed. It is quite a reassuring feeling for me, like a nervous passenger who grabs the seat when an aircraft hits turbulence, momentarily ignoring the fact that the seat is an integral part of the plummeting aircraft that the passenger is riding in. Anyway, the logic dictated that if I pulled the lever hard to go up, when I let it out, I should descend. "Here goes" I thought.

"Shit!"

The loud screeching noise from the engine stopped and was replaced by a sort of whistling sound from the, still turning, propeller. There was also a heavy trembling vibration running through the whole machine as the engine struggled to keep going whilst ticking over. I could not help but notice (normal perception being somewhat raised in these circumstances) that I was going down a lot bloody faster than I went up. I was panicking a bit, unable to find the runaway, when my previous parachuting experience came to my rescue........ I looked down. And there it was, a very real relief I can assure you.

It really was becoming difficult to make out the surface due to the sun disappearing below the horizon and the airfield now covered with an increasingly black shadow. Len must have started to become a little concerned himself as he put on his car headlights which helped illuminate the scabby pot holed runway. I lined up with the runway and continued to descend into the darkness and when nearing the ground, very near in fact, the deckchair landed, seemingly by itself. "Thank the Lord." There was only one minor problem which manifested itself at this time. To give you an idea, have you ever perhaps, as a child, ridden in a shopping trolley? Cast your mind back and recall the little thrill when your parent pushed it faster making you squeal with delight, an early experience of the excitement that

John Clarke

comes with danger. Now imagine you are in that same shopping trolley barrelling along a dark runway with no knowledge of how to stop yourself. I gave a little squeal, I can tell you. Len didn't seem to have noticed me careering towards him but fortunately walked to the side of car as I stopped the flying deckchair abruptly by running into the back of it.

"Sorry" he said, "I forgot to tell you where the brakes are," wistfully looking at the bent parts of the aircraft and the dent in the rear bumper of the Volvo.

"What do you reckon?"" he said hardly hiding his enthusiasm.

"I want one!" I said gleefully.

I would like to pay tribute to Len, as for many years he pushed the boundaries of hang gliding and the new sport of powered hang gliding later named microlighting in many ways. Let me give you just a flavour of the man. In 1979 he was sponsored by Blue Bird Toffees to fly his powered hang glider across the channel to France. The glider in question was powered by a hundred and twenty three cc two stroke engine and flew at twenty five miles per hour. The throttle was a wooden clothes peg which he held in his mouth and had to squeeze tight to rev the engine.

On the day of the flight he started at Potters Bar near London and flew down to Dover where he waited for his ground crew to board a cross channel ferry. He then followed the ferry all the way to France, eventually landing at Abbeville where he was arrested by the Gendarmes. They finally released him after deciding that they couldn't think of law he had actually broken.

What a man.

The People You Meet

Just like those halcyon hang gliding days I also am eternally grateful for being there at the beginning of microlighting. It seems unthinkable today but thirty years ago there were no regulations for flying one's lawn mower powered hang glider. Only when someone flew across the main active runway at Heathrow, without telling anyone beforehand, did The Civil Aviation Authority decide that some regulation was actually required and as a matter of urgency. However back then, I did meet some amazing people involved in the world of powered hang gliding and I recall just two of very many to give you just a flavour of this exciting new and brave world.

Commander Mike was an officer in the Navy and a bit of a pioneering inventor type. He was in his forties, fairly stocky and had the obligatory full naval beard. He, with his team, decided to enter a distance flying competition at the Rifle Range (horrific thoughts come flooding back, as you can possibly imagine) near Mere in Wiltshire. The task was to take off and see who could fly the greatest distance in a straight line in an engineless aircraft.

This site was really quite spectacular. A long, grassy valley with sides four hundred feet high which, at the far end, opened out into the flatlands of Wiltshire. At the other end, where all the flying was to take place, was a natural amphitheatre. I am used to the rough grasslands with a plethora of rocks sticking out of our dramatic limestone scarred uplands but here there wasn't a blade of grass out of place. No sign of rocks just the most beautifully manicured grass, cut so short that you could play crown green bowls on it, except of course it was very steep and one's bowls would end up four hundred feet away at the bottom. When Commander Mike and his platoon appeared at the site on that windless July day he brought his pedal powered Tweetie to win the day. Commander Mike and his aircraft...the Tweetie. You could not make it up.

The Tweetie was less like the usual hang glider shape as it had a bit of a tail plane sticking out at the back, but Commander M's secret weapon was to have a propeller sticking out of the back connected by a long aluminium propshaft to a bicycle chain, bicycle crank and pedals which the noble commander would furiously pedal during flight. This turned the propeller giving additional thrust and extending the flight to secure victory.

To watch him and his ground support team in action was a lesson in a perfect military machine working at its best. For the six members of his ground support team, beautifully turned out in their naval garb, would wordlessly and with well drilled military precision assemble his contraption ready for flight. This took about half an hour. When the craft was ready the Senior Non Commissioned Officer would go around the assembled aircraft doing a thorough pre flight check constantly referring to copious pages on a large clipboard. All this time Commander Mike would stand back and monitor his team's performance, his meticulous concentration not disturbed one iota by the curious gazes and comments of the assembled crowd who had come to watch. Eventually the NCO marched to the Commander saluted and declared the machine fit for flight. The ground crew stood away from the machine and formed up to attention in a perfect straight line. This with the sweat running down their cheeks due to their previous efforts and the increasing heat from the ever climbing sun, not a muscle dared twitch under the stern gaze of their commanding officer and one could only admire their discipline.

Dunge Bottom

Commander Mike then approached the machine with the stomach in chest out posture of a military man, strapped himself in and readied himself for flight and certain victory. The theory was impressive, the machine looked more than impressive and the way it was prepared for the mission was breathtaking. As I looked on I felt a pang of guilt mixed with a great pride that I had never enrolled to serve my country. It was an awe inspiring demonstration of 'Rule Britannia'. The Royal Navy had taken on and defeated all comers. Winning the competition would be a walk in the park. The wind had freshened slightly now which helped the take off a little as pilots did not have to run quite so far and there was also a little bit of hill lift to help them on their respective ways.

A hushed silence fell on the assembled spectators who in the main were pilots themselves and who now gazed in incredulity at the mighty pedalled powered Tweetie. This was the first time that most pilots had seen one our shores. It was an American design and Commander Mike had it shipped over specially to help him win this prestigious competition. He took a deep breath, looked around checking all was clear, and commenced his purposeful run towards the edge. It seemed to take an age before the glider started to support its own weight, presumably because of the propeller, propshaft and bicycle bits, but eventually it did and after a further few committed strides he was airborne.

The Tweetie started a gentle climb as it flew into the rising air in front of the hill, but quickly flew out of the lift and commenced a gentle descending glide towards the grassy ground four hundred feet away. Commander Mike wearing his special harness, found the bicycle pedals and at last started to crank up the propeller until it was but a blur.

John Clarke

At this point the descent was arrested and he was able to maintain height. Gasps of amazement escaped from the mouths of the crowd as it was obvious that the pedalled powered Tweetie would just keep going and going into the distance, easily beating all the other competitors. Victory was assured.

Until the propeller fell off !

It was surreal moment as the propeller descended as gracefully as a sycamore seed pirouettes on its fall to earth. Coincidentally, it was at this moment that Commander Mike began a steep, and somewhat more rapid, descent into the nearby fields. I really felt quite sorry for him. The final ignominy being that the propeller landed after him.

This just seemed to be the way in those days, wacky ideas that defied belief.

I guess even the Navy can't win them all.

Another chap I remember with fondness was Ashley. One day in the middle of August a large number of people, both pilots and interested members of the general public gathered at a disused airfield again somewhere in the deepest depths of Wiltshire, to attend a powered hang gliding Festival of Flight. At this event were also powered hang glider manufacturers all vying to attract attention and secure sales for their embryonic flying machines. One of these was Ashley.

Now Ashley's invention was fabulous for he had attached a lawn mower engine to his normal hang glider and fixed it onto a triangular shaped under carriage made of light weight aluminium. At each corner were fitted wheels, none of which were steerable. It was a scorching summer's day, the sky was dappled with fluffy white cumulus clouds and there was a light but fickle wind. On each side of the old broken stone scattered runway was glowing golden corn standing about six feet tall, a glorious day indeed, bucolic England at its best.

Eventually it was Ashley's turn to show off his machine. He dragged it out onto the rocky runway, started the engine by pulling a length of cord, much like a lawnmower in fact. Ashley's machine varied from the usual setup in as much as the pilot, clipped in the harness, lay flat on the undercarriage trolley. It all looked most promising for we all knew that the hang glider he had chosen was a good one with decent performance. The addition of his engine meant that quality flying would be on the cards. An expectant silence fell on the assembled enthusiasts as we waited for aviation to commence. A growl from the engine and then a rising aggressive tone as it revved up to the maximum. It was a noise like an enormous flock of bees buzzing about in irritation. Initially the aircraft accelerated slowly forward, but gradually going quicker and quicker and quicker until the inevitable take off.

At least that was how it should have gone. What actually happened was that after about twenty yards of trundling down the runway, Ashley and his flying machine hit one of the numerous stones, which caused it to veer off, turning ninety degrees to the left and at now high speed taxied straight into the six foot high standing corn. He completely disappeared from view apart from the aluminium post supporting the top wires of his glider. It looked like something out of Jaws, where you just see the dorsal fin of the Great White Shark cutting through the swell as it circles its victim. The king post of his glider was similarly scything through the standing corn causing sheaves to be thrown up and back, all the while to the accompaniment of the loud buzzing noise of the harassed bees.

Everyone fully expected Ashley to cut the engine and

bring this most amusing, but embarrassing, situation under control. But no, Ashley was made of sterner stuff for with the engine still screaming at maximum speed he turned through one hundred and eighty degrees having hit another rock in the field. He then reappeared briefly on the runway as he crossed over into the corn on the other side. The Jaws effect continued as he disappeared off into the distance, only to eventually fade from view, with just an increasingly faint buzzing noise to let us know that Ashley was still making efforts to fly. In fact for the next forty minutes whilst other exhibitors were demonstrating their wares Ashley would keep appearing and reappearing randomly at various places on the airfield.

Later, he finally returned to confirm that the throttle had jammed wide open and he couldn't close it down despite his best endeavours and the only reason he hadn't completed mowing the corn was because he had at last run out of fuel.

Before I move on I have to mention one person I would have loved to have met. He was a chap I mentioned earlier, the intriguingly named Percy Pilcher. He was born in 1866 in Bath and became a pupil of the gliding great Otto Lillienthal. Now, when you think of pioneering powered flight the Wright Brothers are probably the first names that spring to mind and yet, but for a tragic twist of fate, it should have been the Pilcher name that conquered all. Percy was convinced that heavier than air, powered flight could be achieved and he managed to design a triplane that was steerable and powered by a four horsepower engine. The year was 1899 and creating engines was an expensive business so Percy went in search of sponsorship. A show flight was set up, but a few days before the businessmen were due to turn up the crankshaft on the engine broke.

Dunge Bottom

Not wishing to let down the sponsors and lose a potentially lucrative deal Percy decided to demonstrate one of his gliders instead, a beautiful craft he had christened 'The Hawk'. On the day of the test the weather was poor but our intrepid Englishman flew anyway and, you may have seen this coming, crashed. The hawk survived and can now been seen in the National Museum of Scotland, however, Percy did not and now the only concrete reminder of him is a small column in a field in Lutterworth, Leicestershire, the site of the accident. "So what?" I can hear you saying. "This crashing thing is all a bit too common in the ultralight flying fraternity." Well, that was true, but the remarkable thing is, Percy had it right. In 2003 engineers from Cranfield University used Pilcher's plan and built a replica of his machine. They achieved a powered, controlled flight of one minute twenty five seconds, a full twenty seconds longer than the Wright Brother attained in 1903. Had he have lived people would have asked "Orville and Wilbur who?" and the genesis of powered flight would have belonged to a man called Percy.

7

Gerald, a Parachute and a Plastic Pig

I was very fortunate to know a really lovely eccentric
schoolteacher called Gerald, who was always full to the
brim with enthusiasm for absolutely everything, especially
flying. I met him through the local hang gliding club initially,
but we mostly met at the three sites which were fairly close
to where he lived. In fact, in my mind and it may only be
my mind, he was the one who started the sport of
paragliding off hills in this country. Paragliding, boiled down
to its essence, is leaping off hills with an already inflated
parachute above your head so that you can fly around. Up
until this point parachutes had been used exclusively for
leaping out of an aeroplane with the purpose of saving life
if the aircraft became unserviceable. This developed into
people leaping out of aircraft for fun, regardless of its
condition. Some folks had an idea about trying to do the
same off hills but nothing much seemed to be coming of it
at the time, until Gerald got his prominent teeth into the

Dunge Bottom

idea. The paragliders used nowadays have a big wing area and, as a consequence, really high performance. Unfortunately when Gerald decided to invent the sport there were no such big parachutes so he had to make do with the very small free fall type parachute that skydivers used. The disadvantage with these was that they came down through the air very quickly (because they were small) and their descent angle was very steep, about one foot forward to about three foot down.

I was at Edge Top one day waiting for the wind to pick up when he came over to me and whispered,

"Do you want a trip?" My mind raced, what could he mean, surely it was too early in the season for magic mushrooms? I looked into his wide staring eyes, with spectacles canted at an impossible angle due, I suspect, to his extra large unlevelled ears. His appearance seemed to confirm my suspicions about magic mushrooms. He must have sensed my musings and delayed response for he continued,

"On my parachute idiot", he muttered.

"What parachute Gerald?" I innocently enquired.

"This one" he replied showing me a bundle of green and brown nylon, with grubby bits of cord festooned from various parts of it. It certainly looked nothing like any parachute I had seen before.

"I'm just developing it" he whispered, "everything's got to be hush hush." I sighed and hoped that the other thirty or so pilots at Edge Top at that moment could not hear what was going on. Still, always game for a new adventure I agreed readily and went through the briefing...

"Run as hard as you can into wind and down the very steep slope, fly over the walls and land in the fields at the bottom"

John Clarke

Gerald said. "If you are lucky with this wind you might just stay up and soar along the front of the ridge."

"Sounds good, you managed it yet?" I enquired innocently.

"Not as such" was the hushed reply.

Now just to let you know, Edge Top's slope is in fact about one in three. At the bottom, which is about two hundred feet down, there was a large stone wall next to a farm track, another large stone wall, followed a by large sloping fields leading down to the small stream far below in the valley bottom. Although, given my previous experiences, you would think I would have known better, I looked at the rig, and the slope and a strange dreaming optimism washed over me. Some people get an adrenaline rush, some people need to push boundaries. I was just a moron. The words "Let's have a go" fell like dribble from my lips.

The waiting pilots had by now realized that something unusual was going on and started to pay attention. They soon saw me charging towards the edge of this very steep hill dragging a mucky green and brown bag of what looked like washing behind me as I disappeared from view. From my perspective, I felt that what they saw was what I experienced, namely running as hard as I can towards the edge of the ridge and...disappearing downwards!

I was now in the situation where I was running as hard as I could down this slope, with this large wall fast approaching looking worryingly solid. I remembered my very earliest days at hang gliding at the Rifle Range. The parachute was supposed to slow me down and I remember thinking how annoying this would be if I was leaping from my burning Sopwith. It was actually quite annoying anyway as the wall was approaching and I was suffering a distinct lack of flight.

Dunge Bottom

I took a blind leap of faith, and just missed the wall only to skid into the farm track at an embarrassingly high rate of knots, with the second wall luckily stopping any further progress. I was unsure as to how my hill credibility would survive this as I was now lying in crumpled heap covered by this tiny parachute listening to Gerald's rapid descent down the slope.

"That was brilliant John" says Gerald, "I've not been able to get that high on any of my efforts here" he grinned gleefully. "I really think that I'm getting somewhere now". He was laughing like a crazed professor with a new vaporising laser. "See you cracked your shins there, do you want another go?" he asked. I really like Gerald and but my legs were bleeding and was struggling with immense pain that turned my vision red. I was also struggling with survivor trauma and the feeling that somehow I no longer deserved to be alive.

"No thanks Gerald" I said quietly. At this he packed away his flying machine in its green and brown rucksack and left the hill with obvious pride and satisfaction that he was really making serious headway in this embryonic sport.

On another occasion, I was fortunate enough to be soaring high above Edge Top one December day. The sun shone in clear blue sky, deep snow lay on the ground and the chilled but invigorating air heightened the senses. I could see for miles in the crystal clear air, and the wind was so smooth it was like flying in cream. I felt like I could fly forever in any direction without ever landing. I didn't have to physically move to turn the glider, I just had to think it and round it went. Ah magic. So it was truly a rare and special day that every now again turned up…usually on Mondays.

The road along the ridge was deep in snow but the car

John Clarke

tyres from the other pilots had cut tracks in the road to enable everyone to reach the site, apart from...Gerald. You see, he drove a plastic pig, as they were affectionately known. More properly a Reliant Robin, a three wheel car with one wheel at the front, in the centre and two at the back, with the body being made out of fibreglass. As I flew high above the ridge I saw Gerald approaching in his plastic pig from the main road which had been cleared by the snow ploughs. All was going well until he reached our narrow lane. He simply stopped. The problem was that all the previous cars had four wheels so the tracks were cut in the snow at the sides of the cars. Gerald's pig had the front wheel in the middle where the snow hadn't been cleared. For the next hour, watching from my vantage point high in the azure sky, I saw Gerald butting his Pig up against the snow drifts in a vain attempt to reach the site. I could imagine his frustration at failing so comprehensively to reach the site which was tantalizingly just out of reach. All made worse by seeing us flying so high and free far above him.

I never knew Gerald to swear ever, but I do wonder if at this one time he didn't just let out the odd gentle expletive. He never did make it. Eventually he slowly, sadly turned around like a wounded animal and slunk back towards civilization. It reminded me of salmon trying to leap weirs in an effort to reach the spawning grounds ...and failing; only to return unfulfilled to the sea. So sad. We often reminded Gerald of that day, possibly not kindly because flying days like that in winter are few are far between. He always took it good part by scowling and walking away with head held high. Humans can be so cruel. However, things actually deteriorated even more for Gerald and his pig.

We were all flying at Mam Tor, one glorious summer

day. It end of it we carried our gliders down the track at the back of was another red letter day and all had some great flights. At the end of it we carried out gliders down the track at the back of the hill where we had parked some of the cars, Gerald's pig included. The job of tying the gliders onto the roof racks continued with well practiced ease, when someone was heard to ask of Gerald.....

"Can you smell anything?"

"No" replied Gerald.

"You can't smell burning then?"

"No" said Gerald again.

It was at this point when a number of pilots began to confirm that they too could smell burning.

"Have you started smoking Gerald?" asked another.

"Certainly not" asserted Gerald

"Have you got a fire extinguisher in your pig Gerald?" asked the original questioner.

"No, why?" was his confused reply.

"Cos your pigs on fire!"

"Oh Gosh" was Gerald's measured response. It was true, somehow or other Gerald's pig had caught fire and was now literally beginning to melt in front of our assembled eyes and spreading like molten tar all over the lay by.

When the sacrificial melt had finally finished all that was left visible of Gerald's Pig, was the engine and the metal seat frames, sitting in a depressed puddle of liquid plastic.

We did feel for Gerald at this time for the poor chap just stood staring in silence at his dead pig. He did not swear or curse, or rage and beat his chest in anger and frustration, he did not blame anyone, or call on the Lord, just this bowed shouldered silence with hands hanging

John Clarke

limply at his side. After what seemed an endless silence, Gerald finally turned away from his pig, muttered almost inaudibly, "Oh Dear" and slowly started to trudge a lonely furrow homeward.

8
A Microlight, A Parachute and Tomorrow's World

You see I had a friend called Len the Car (no not that one, a second hand car salesman) and one called Pete; who between them had a cunning plan. I met them both through hang gliding as they both shared the same passion for flying foot launched gliders. I got to know Len the Car very well as he lived fairly close by at a beautiful hall he and his partner Bobbie had bought at auction sometime ago. It was nestled on the side of Monsal Dale and was picture perfect with stunning views over the Wye valley which wandered through the dale below. Len the Car and Bobbie ran the hall as bed and breakfast and Len sold hang gliders, spares and general flying accessories from there, as well as running a second hand car showroom in Rotherham. Now Len and I are of similar age and height but he had the ability to sell something, no matter how inconsequential to all who visited the Hall. It was magic just to watch him, one day, sell an altimeter to the chimney sweep who had arrived to clean the huge chimney in the West Wing and who had never flown in his life. Still, those brushes can go up high....I suppose.

Anyway, Len the Car and Pete had a parachute. Pete was a slightly built man who came from Mexborough and who had the most outrageous accent. He was mostly incomprehensible, with a wicked sense of humour, I think, although due to his accent, it was difficult to be sure. Len and Pete had an idea about marrying a parachute and microlight together so that should disaster befall a microlight in flight then their parachute system would bring both the pilot and the aircraft down to earth safely.

One day Len and I were sitting at Bradwell Edge, a long ridge overlooking a cement factory, waiting for the wind to pick up/slow down/change direction.

"Have you still got your microlight?" he asked, out of the blue.

"Yes" I confirmed except it wasn't strictly mine as I had half share in it with someone else. Len the Car then started to explain their ideas and it was obvious he was becoming more and more enthusiastic about the project the longer he talked. As I listened I realised that this was not just the famous Len the Car sales patter, he was genuinely enthused about the project. So much so that what he was telling me infected me like a virus.

"Is there any way I can get in on this" I asked him directly.

"Oh sure" A smile crept across his lips and I wondered, for a split second, if I had been suckered after all.

"We need some help with the test flying" he said, looking out over the valley.

John Clarke

I wondered if I'd just been sold a Lada Riva Sport....that I didn't really need.

Initially all I had to do was allow them to fix a two foot long torpedo shaped thing at the back of the microlight. Inside was a twenty eight foot diameter parachute sitting on top of an enormous spring. Once this was done I would taxi along the old battered runway at Ashbourne and pull the release mechanism, which was a D shaped metal handle attached to the end of the torpedo. When I pulled the handle the end cap released and the spring blasted out the parachute. We had many such sessions testing the system and it went really well, so we graduated to repeating the procedure while flying at various heights. At this point he parachute was not actually fixed to the microlight so it was just ejected behind me to fall back down to the ground, whereupon I would land normally.

We were now getting to a point where a real live deployment was required to completely prove the system and hopefully encourage microlight pilots to shell out a few quid and buy it. Len the Car applied his sales magic and managed to get the television programme, Tomorrows World, interested. They booked a day in late November to come out to Ashbourne and film the whole thing which would give us the national publicity we needed. We were all obviously very excited and yet at the same time apprehensive. To be more accurate, Len the Car and Pete were excited, I was apprehensive as I was going to be the one who actually went up there to do it. After long and detailed discussion we decided that a dress rehearsal would be a good idea prior to the visit from the Tomorrows World Team, so it was all agreed that we would meet up the next Friday afternoon at the airfield and try it all out for real.

Friday afternoon arrived all too soon, for me anyway, as

Dunge Bottom

I was becoming increasingly nervous. There had been a hard frost overnight and the ground was solid despite the weak watery sun doing its best to warm things up. It was a strange motley collection of people that assembled that afternoon on the bleak expanse of the frozen airfield, me of course with the microlight, Len the Car and Pete, the other Len of Skyhook fame who was there to use his micro light to fly around and film the whole thing from the air, Charlie who often flew with me and his daughter Kate, who were going to photograph things from the ground

The plan was for the other Len Gabriels to take off first to get into position for his filming. I would then take off and climb to two thousand feet. Once I was ready I would switch off the engine then pull the ripcord to activate the parachute and descend safely and gently to earth. We had taken safety very seriously so I was equipped with a brand new pair of gloves and a radio, so that I could be updated on progress from the ground. We also had an escape plan if things really didn't work out. Once the parachute had deployed the microlight would be descending slightly nose down and if I felt all was not going well then I had a quick release to free me from the parachute. I could then dive and pick up speed before gliding down to land. I was reassured to hear from the all the assembled throng that this would definitely happen so don't worry, but perhaps the decision height about cutting away the parachute should be about five hundred feet.

Wondering quite how I had got here I found myself lined up at the end of the runway, with the trusty two stroke engine thrumming away behind me. I looked around nervously hoping that perhaps Len the Car and Pete had changed their minds and thought about cancelling the whole thing. No all I was getting was encouraging smiles and the "thumbs up" from all and sundry. It is strange what adrenaline can do because I did not notice the cold only the brightness of the sun low in the sky causing me to squint against its rays.

I could not delay things further so with gritted teeth I opened the throttle and accelerated over the rutted frozen surface of the runway. It took about thirty seconds before I had built up enough speed to leave the ground and reach for the chilly emptiness of that winter's sky. Steadily I climbed until I reached the desired two thousand feet. The view that met me was something akin to a Turner painting as everywhere I looked the land was painted in gently whispered hues of winter colours softened by the wash of the watery sun. I looked around to check on the position of the Len in the camera aircraft before making sure I was over the correct part of the airfield. I called over the radio for the go ahead. The static from the radio was very loud but completely garbled. I did think about quitting at this point but the enthusiasm of the others played on my conscience, after all I owed it to these guys to do what I said I would.

With one final look around I took a deep breath and with my left hand I flicked the switch which killed the engine. The silence was eerie and for the first time I became aware of the icy wind hitting my face. With my right hand I reached for the ripcord which would open the parachute. As it blew out behind me I felt an enormous sensation of stopping. The nose of the micro light dipped down and I started my descent. There was a loud crackling from the radio, which I couldn't understand it at all.

"Still, got my new gloves so should be okay", I thought. I was starting to relax a little and had chance to look around now and noticed Len flying around, even smiling as he waved to me. Then things got a little worse. After dropping

Dunge Bottom

about seven hundred and fifty feet, the microlight started swinging from side to side with increasing intensity. The situation was uncomfortable but I felt I was doing something genuinely pioneering and I needed to stick it out as long as possible. Despite this, by the time I got to six hundred feet things were very uncomfortable and I was concerned that the micro light would be wiped out, along with me, on landing. It was decision time. I remembered what the team had said, just dive, pick up flying speed, fly down and land. I made the decision and gave the release cord a firm tug.

Instantly there was a loud twanging sound, and the unstoppable force of the control bar of the glider coming back into my stomach. This however paled into insignificance to what happened next.

The microlight turned completely upside down. I was deafened by the loud cracking sounds as both wing tubes broke, followed in rapid succession by both cross tubes. The sail now enveloped me like a shroud. I was completely blind, upside down and falling. This happened in less than a second. I did not know what to do. The foetal position seemed the obvious thing and despite the seatbelt securing me to the microlight, I curled up into ball and waited. I do remember thinking to myself, in a very calm way.

"Oh dear this is going to hurt"

I have since watched numerous movies where the bad guy falls screaming and cursing from the mountain/ skyscraper/ aircraft but the reality is, you don't. If anything I was too overcome by the realization that I was completely helpless. As was later calculated by measuring the video footage I was plummeting vertically towards the frozen ground at about sixty miles per hour. It was only the drag from the sail was helping keep my speed down. I could not see out so I did not know when the ground would arrive, only that, most certainly, it would. This was quite reassuring as it reminded me of my first high flights off Bunster hill on my hang glider when the crash helmet was pushed forward over my eyes. A strangely comforting thought.

The impact was shockingly heavy and accompanied by a very sharp cracking sound from my right arm giving me a clue as to the subsequent fracture. The sharp pain in my pelvis also made me suspect that I might have a problem in that area. "Fractured bones are on the cards here" I thought. Looking on the bright side I wasn't knocked out and as I systematically wiggled my toes and fingers I thought that at least my spine was okay.

Wrong again, but that's another story.

I still couldn't see anything of course so I lay there, waiting for help to arrive. I soon heard hesitant steps drawing nearer. When the steps paused I managed to lift the sail up with my good arm only to see Pete looking very pale with wide staring eyes. My immediate concern was that he might faint, fall and hurt himself. I told him to sit down and hold his head between his legs and breath slowly. Others soon arrived and I was able to reassure them that I was okay, apart from the rather severe pain in my pelvis and serious discomfort from the arm, but I counted these as minor inconveniences compared with how I could have been at this point. I lay on the frozen ground for what seemed quite a long time, probably because it was quite a long time, about half an hour in fact, and I was getting colder and colder all the time. No one dared move me in case it made my injuries worse.

Eventually the ambulance arrived along with police and fire service. It would appear that the call they received was that an aircraft had crashed on the airfield, hence all the excitement. The fire service was particularly disappointed due to no fire and no need to cut me out of the wreckage, so they left in high dudgeon! The ambulance crew was deciding how near they could get their vehicle on the frozen grass. They didn't want to carry me any further than necessary of course. The police officer seemed the most bemused as no one would talk to him. Eventually he cornered Pete (which is not easy in the middle of a field) and tried to ask him for some details. I can only say that I very much admired the police officer's persistence in questioning Pete as his accent was even more indecipherable due, presumably, to increased stress levels

"Where did he come from?" asked the police officer. Pete, looking at the police officer with complete amazement, hesitated and pointed upwards

"From up there" I did feel sorry for this unfortunate member of the constabulary who at that point disappeared muttering under his breath.

Shortly afterwards, the ambulance crew casually returned and suggested that with their help I should stand up and walk to the ambulance. I did point out my broken arm and the pain in my pelvis. I also perhaps naively muttered about had they got anything for the pain which was inexorably worsening with time.

"Oh no, you'll have to wait until we've got you on the ambulance mate. Up you get then." they cheerfully encouraged me. Their reassuring banter continued by telling me not to rush, to take my time and they would support me under my arms. Oh and by the way could I hold my broken arm with my good one?

Silly clumsy old me, because whilst trying to get up I experienced excruciating pain somewhere within my pelvic girdle which caused me to let go of my broken arm which consequently fell back onto the ground. This was followed by further excruciating pain which shot down the full length of my arm into my fingers. Anyway, we made it into the back of the ambulance with no further damage and was told to lie down on the stretcher. I again enquired about some pain relief because I didn't want to blub in front of these professional medics. Grudgingly they offered me gas and air, or laughing gas as it is affectionately called. I suspect that my gas and air was faulty as I didn't laugh once. We then started off at a very slow speed towards the Derbyshire Royal Infirmary. I again asked if they couldn't go a bit faster as I really was about to cry anytime soon.

"Oh no, we only go quickly for people who are really hurt,"

I felt duly chastened and rebuked at this selfishness on my part and vowed not to bother them again during the journey. I couldn't help but wonder however if their definition of seriously hurt and mine would ever converge.

My time at the Derby Royal Infirmary that evening was very hazy due mainly to the injections of morphine I was receiving. In fact I was told later that I had been rushed into the X-ray Dept upon arrival as they couldn't believe that anyone having fallen five hundred feet didn't have numerous fractures especially to the spine and neck. After some one and a half hours of X- raying they declared that there was no damage to my back at all. How lucky was that. They simply found a fractured upper right arm with possible nerve damage. It took another eighteen months to find that I had actually fractured my spine as well.

Still could have been much worse eh!

Due to the injuries I was unable to work for a little while. This was, in a strange way, very fortunate because during that time, I learnt to fly powered aircraft, gaining my Private

Pilot's Licence and continued to fly sailplanes. I also met, and fell in love with, my Physiotherapist, (beautiful eyes, lovely hair, perfect smile and a fabulous bottom).

So really it all turned out for the best.

It's Okay I Ran Him Over

Mr. Burke the surgeon, at the Derby Royal Infirmary monitored my physical failings for three months with me taking regular trips to the hospital to visit his clinic. He was a lovely friendly sort of a chap who listened carefully to my repetitive moans about not getting better until finally he decided that I should have some physiotherapy to help mobilize my now healed arm and so sent me off to Burton District Hospital.

About two weeks later I found myself waiting in the bustling main reception area of the hospital, amusing myself trying to guess which staff member would come for me. I was somewhat concerned as most of the staff seemed to wear their moustaches with obvious pride, except the men, of course, who were clean shaven. A young lady appeared, sans moustachio, and dressed rather fetchingly in a white uniform tunic trimmed with blue (which matched the colour of her eyes), dark blue trousers and shoulder length chestnutty brown hair.

"Hello, I'm Pam" said The Vision with a lovely smile, the incandescent gleam of the fluorescent lights reflecting powerfully from her pearl white teeth

"Would you like to follow me down to the Gym?"

"Oh yes" I thought. I admit to having tunnel vision at this point as I couldn't focus on anything other than her bottom, ricocheting off the walls of th ecorridor. I was only glad that she didn't cast a backwards glance. It really was a most exquisite derriere, I do remember thinking and still is, dear. "Yep she's the one!" I thought to myself. However, it did take some time and inventive wooing for her to reciprocate those feelings.

Having sat down at a desk full of paperwork she explained that this would be an assessment session prior to actual treatment. No problems then. I was pleased at the thought of having no pain today! The Vision took the normal sort of details and then stood up muttering about having to go and get a goneometer. This didn't sound too good, why on earth would she need to measure my gonads? I mean here I was in broad daylight in the middle of a gymnasium and a beautiful young woman who I had only just met wants to measure my gonads. Can the stories that I had previously heard about Physios be true? They are obsessed by the body beautiful to the exclusion of all else. "Bloody hell." I know that size is not allegedly important, but my particular gonads had never really recovered following my parachuting escapades and had seldom see the light of day. Anyway, what were they to do with my arm? I needed to get out of here but my escape route was down the same corridor and I would be seen by the woman I most needed to impress.

"Bugger."

I needed to try and calm down, after all she could not use the goneometer on me without my permission could she? I relaxed a little and casually glanced at the paper and files strewn desk in front of me when I noticed a name that was familiar.

"Bloody hell" I said, out loud, "I know him"

I started to read these notes about Duane, who was in hospital with two broken legs. I was absorbed in the details when The Vision returned. I have to admit she was not best pleased to find me reading someone else's notes. I am led to believe that you are not supposed to read your own notes let alone someone else's.

She was furious. Five minutes into our relationship and we were going to have our first argument. This was not a good start. I could tell she was about to castigate me soundly, as her a face turned black as thunder, which in another time and place I might have found rather attractive, slamming the goneometer down on the desk, her mouth opened ready to spew vitriol upon my defenceless soul. Just in time I spluttered

"It's okay, I know him. I ran him over" At this utterance she stopped, looked at me oddly and paused long enough for me to tell her the sequence of events that caused me to know Duane.

I had just fetched my Toyota van back from the spray shop in down town Burton having been resprayed. It looked lovely, all shiny and blue and I thought the not inconsiderable amount I had forked out was money well spent. As I was almost home having covered all of two miles a young git on a motorbike tried to overtake where there wasn't enough room. He scraped himself down the side of my lovely new paint job and fell off in front of me.

"Bastard" the word just fell from my lips.

Fortunately I was not able to stop in time and ran over him.

Hence the two broken legs.

Later, when I had to go to court as a witness to this tragic event Duane forget to attend the hearing and we all had to wait whilst the police went to his house, woke him up and dragged him into the court room. It was then discovered that Duane had not only forgotten to attend but had also forgotten to bring his driving licence with him as previously

John Clarke

requested. This gives you an idea about Duane the person, I'm sure. The fates were kind to me as the Vision, having treated him already, had the measure of the lad, and could confirm he was indeed a young git and I suspect she reluctantly decided to let me off the ritual castigation, for which I am eternally grateful.

Anyhow, over the next few weeks I visited PJ (I was now allowed to call her this rather than "The Vision") in an attempt to mobilize the elbow which was rather seized up through a long spell of inactivity.

She at first thought me a wimp as every time she tried to increase the range of movements I would let out a little whimper, even a loud cry and one or more tears, following the production of a loud cracking sound coming from somewhere deep within my upper arm. My reputation was only saved because of the enormous zits covering my upper right arm. Apparently the nerve damage had altered things somehow to produce such a mighty crop of pustules. These were not one's ordinary spots, which were inconsequential by comparison. No these were of Versuvian proportions, I suspected that at that moment the only Earthly things that could be viewed from space were the Great Wall of China and the zits covering my limb. They needed handling with delicacy because if one had accidentally gone off without exercising the required care and attention, then toxic waste would have laid parts of the hospital complex out of bounds for years. Fortunately I was in the hands of a professional who understood the mechanism of such things and handled them with aplomb and obvious delight. Mind you I suspect that even she was incredulous at seeing how far the super charged pus could actually travel. And I can confirm that this was indeed a mighty distance. I shared her enthusiasm vicariously as due to the nerve damage in my arm I could only see the eruptions without actually feeling the pleasurable agony as the things went off.

She also had the mischievous knack of tickling my upper right arm which caused the fingers of my right to itch, very strange and I suspect once again attractive to her? It would seem that I was rapidly becoming legend within the hospital, as, whilst receiving this "special treatment" various members of staff would just "pop in" to have a look.

I needed some form of special attraction, to win PJ's affections: since I had been inactive for such a long time and had developed a "wobble" and certainly wasn't looking my best. I knew she was "the one" but strangely it wasn't reciprocated yet and what was worse she was actually engaged(ish) – bugger! She also mentioned that she couldn't be interested in any of her patients (something to do with professional standards and ethics), or a divorcé, which I had managed to become in my former time. My only saving grace apart from my zits, and being slightly odd compared to her normal patients, was that I seemed to have the ability to make her laugh, not only at me but just occasionally with me, and dare I suggest that she came to look forward to my visits. However, despite this things were really not looking too hopeful, nay, dare I say they looked bleak.

A plan was needed for a successful wooing and this is what I came up with:

1. The zits, I mean no one could compete with mine and after studying such things over my current lifetime I now realize that ladies in general are fascinated by blackheads and zits. So I was onto a definite winner here.

2. Perhaps talks of daring-do with my flying exploits, (I was still flying gliders with my one arm and also had nearly finished training for my private pilot's licence).

3. Make her giggle.

John Clarke

4. Make a description of the drainage system of the hospital both informative and amusing all at the same time. Not as easy as it sounds I assure you.

5. Wear my father's shoes.

6. Stop being a patient.

Number five may seem strange but on one particular visit I had, for some reason, borrowed a pair of my father's shoes which she remarked upon favourably. After feeling the cracking in my upper arm again and sneering at the whimpering sounds emanating from my direction she decided to discharge me from her care (brilliant point six achieved) and pack me off to see Mr. Burke, again just to check things out.

So once again I found myself in fear and trembling in Mr. Burke's clinic being examined by his burly rugby playing Australian Houseman who when jiggling my arm produced the same whimper, cracking sound and tears that PJ had been experiencing over the last few weeks. After a little chat between Mr Burke and his Houseman it was decided that perhaps my arm had not in fact healed and was being rebroken every time I was subjected to physio treatment.

"Time to operate John M'boy" smiled Mr. Burke. "We'll get you in as soon as we can, probably a couple of weeks."

He went on to explain that the radial nerve in my arm was not going to recover on its own now so he would need to replace it with a nerve from my leg which should resolve the problem of my arm and hand not working . He also said that they would put a plate in my arm to join the bone as it had obviously not knitted together as it should either. He was very jolly about this and made it all sound so straightforward, it couldn't happen soon enough. I have to admit that when I popped in to see PJ, just to let her know how I got on with Mr. Burke, I couldn't help but play the

123

martyr. I only mentioned ad nauseum that PJ had been breaking my arm three times a week for some weeks and that she shouldn't feel too guilty, honestly!

Now I was no longer a patient I felt able to up the wooing levels with PJ., who I suspect officially viewed me as a non patient and therefore might consider extracurricular activities if I could only come up with something original and inventive. I also had plenty of time as I was still unable to work so could merely play at gliding and continue to learn how to fly powered aircraft. My big opportunity arose when I heard that she was intending to move into her new flat.

You see, it didn't stop me trying the typical young lothario techniques, you know arriving at her new flat where she had only moved in the night before with the aid of a mate and her sort of fiancé, I'm not that stupid, let the grunts do all the work.

I arrived in a blood red Lotus Eclat sports car, with biscuit coloured (that's a sort of creamy beige colour, not hob nob coloured – I mention this for the removal of doubt) leather seats, clutching a dozen red roses, a bottle of Asti Spumante (don't you just love that name?) and a chocolate.

Actually I had started out with quite a large number of chocolates, but you know what it's like when you are nervous, you just have to nibble away at something and in this case it was PJ's chocolates. Any how, I was greeted warmly, then slightly less warmly when the number of chocolate was revealed and then with pure ridicule when she looked out of her window to see my carriage of love – the Lotus! I remember feeling a little peeved since I had gone all the way up to Doncaster to borrow the bloody thing from Len the car so I could make an impression. In this respect I had succeeded as indeed PJ was impressed but perhaps not quite in the way I had hoped for, you see I was still young and knew nothing of hip injuries and foolishly thought that this would impress her. I too casually glanced out of the window and saw, a sexy bright red lotus, basking in sunlight, around which the pavements still glistened with the early morning dew, adding to the surreal effect was the smokiness of the steam sensually stroking the curves of the body, whilst having the appearance of rising out of the emerald green sea. I'm not sure I didn't catch a faint exotic perfume wafting towards me on the balmy morning air, myrrh or cardigan perhaps.........................

It was a magnificent sight!! Rather like the way the car manufacturers launch a brand new model at the motor show. You know on a rotating stand, draped with girls and dry ice covering all in soft focus.

Reality hit me like a sledge hammer!!

"Bloody Hell"...I dashed down to the car and gazed in awe as my best laid plans were destroyed by bloody Lotus reliability… the water pump had fallen off and water was pouring out of the hole in the engine where it used to live and there was an enormous puddle of green radiator water under the car, supported by steam. Oh, I really don't know what you might now think of me. I've just read what I have written, what hallucinogenic trip was I on for pity's sake?

I can only surmise that I was enjoying the tripping effects of accidentally taking an extra Haliborange Vitamin C tablet this morning. There can be no other explanation dear reader. I take one every day which may explain why I am who I am. If I may divert for one moment, it is often said that we are a product of our upbringing. Allow me to tell you a little about mine. It was my late dear departed mother who was the one who introduced me to the Haliborange range of fringe 'medifications' as she used to say. She

Dunge Bottom

enjoyed ill health for many years. Just to clarify this point, she really did enjoy ill health as I remember when her cellulitis arrived she was so happy and as for the quinsy, well that brought an almost psychotic euphoric interval. Anyway what I was going to relate was that she shunned the medical world in favour of fringe medicine and her favourite was Dr. J. Collis Browne's Medical Compound, for all ailments. It was a disgusting brown liquid which was dripped into water and drunk. I suspect its main constituent was a tincture of tar. We took my parents on holiday to a Greek Island one year when they were both in their late seventies. It was lovely to see them both paddling up to their knees in the warm Aegean sea, mother, arm linked with Dad and her walking stick in her other hand. However what I was going to recount was that one breakfast time, Pam and I joined them for breakfast and whilst waiting to be served, the usual morning pleasantries took place.......

"Did you sleep well dears?" asked mother.

I foolishly said that my bottom seemed to not quite be right, obviously not wishing to go into too much detail over breakfast of course.

"Oh dear, try a couple of drops of this" she said handing over the Dr. J. Collis Brownes Medical Compound. Under her watchful eyes, (well to be strictly honest it was one eye as the other had a well developed cataract) I duly took the vile stuff. It was easier to give in and do as she suggested otherwise it would remain the only topic of conversation for the entire day. After a little while, chatting away just before the arrival of the toast, I enquired why was it that foreign water made one constipated.

"I'm sorry dear what did you say? " she spluttered over her cup of tea.

"I was talking about constipation on holiday mother dear"

"Oh dear, you're not constipated are you?" was the immediate response.

"Yes dear"

"Oh dear, oh dear" She looked most uncomfortable at this point.

"Take four of these dear and quickly" she stuttered as she handed over some other strange 'medifications'. It turned out that she had thought that I was referring to diarrhoea initially, not constipation. Therefore the initial dose of two drops of Dr. J. Collis Brownes Medical Compound would have sorted out the diarrhoea but obviously made the constipation far worse, hence the antidote of double the dose of the Acme Stomach Cleansing Balm.

Back to the story ....Time continued to hang heavily whilst waiting for my body bits to heal, relieved only by the continuing powered flying training and gliding as well of course as my pursuit of PJ.

9

Mister Men and Lupins

As I had failed miserably with the wooing of PJ following the Lotus debacle I thought that I needed to be a little more adventurous, so came up with a cunning plan.

Now Len, you know the secondhand car salesman, happened to own a magnificent country house in one of the prettiest Derbyshire Dales, so after some lengthy negotiations I was able to formulate a plan that could not possibly fail. I recount to you as best I can dear reader, the ensuing conversation with PJ.

"Fancy coming away for a week end up in the Dales" I innocently asked of said PJ. one day whilst suffering ritual abuse at the hospital.

"Might do" was the initially disappointing response.

"There'll be no hanky panky" she confirmed.

"If I do come it will be as friends, purely platonic" she further confirmed.

Dunge Bottom

There was a pause in the conversation at this juncture as I desperately tried to remember what the hell platonic meant. I was a failed Grammar School product after all. After sometime trying to decide if there was any encouraging sexual connotation involved I assumed rightly so that there was none.

Bugger.

"I'll expect separate rooms" she further encouraged. I decided to take command of the situation at this point.

"You can have a separate wing if you like. I am going there to open up the house for the season. I will have the East Wing and you can have the West Wing, there are much better views over the valley from there" She stopped and looked at me at this point. Was I winding her up, was it a ploy to attempt a raid on certain under garments? I kept a straight face. She looked unsure as to the level of my cunning. Could I possibly own a country house after all? I do believe that curiosity killed the cat premise worked here as she said that OK she would like to come, but no Hanky Panky mind.

A result.

So as arranged, I picked her up on Friday evening in my swanky black BMW (going for German reliability here – forget Lotus) Except the cam shaft was knackered so we had to have to radio turned up very loud to drown out the appalling clattering noise coming from the engine. Have you ever noticed that ladies, bless them, invariably have to fiddle with the music system of any car, presumably as their way exercising control? Well true to form PJ decided that she wasn't happy with Val Doonican's Greatest Hits, so tried to change over to the radio.

Strange to relate the mighty Blaupunkt music system, immediately self destructed and was never to work again. I don't know why I didn't take this a warning at the time. PJ is nothing if not consistent as I have since found out. We spent a happy hour or so chattering away, accompanied by the engine clattering away, until we arrived at the Hall. Silently now, (that is apart from the clattering engine of course), our voices hushed, we approached from high above, down a long winding gravel drive to park in front of the magnificent Gothic styled Hall, with magnificent views of the dale forming a film set like backdrop.

Standing on the raised entrance were two menial servant types, forming a guard of honour (albeit a small one). They were dressed like characters from a Dickens novel and pulled respectful forelocks as we approached.

"Welcome young Sir " "We hope the house is to your satisfaction. Is this young lady your guest?"

"Be so good to take the young ladies things to the West Wing" I barked out.

"Immediately Sir"

I glanced across at PJ to try and gauge the reaction to this previously rehearsed scene. You see Len and Bobbie were playing at being Mr. and Mrs. Lurch and by jiminy they were very convincing indeed.

I could see that she was almost in a state of belief, what a plan. "How could my evil intent fail now?" I thought foolishly. Well actually it could and fail very easily on two counts:

1. PJ although possibly impressed would not weaken for such materialistic trinkets and

2. Mr. Lurch loudly saying.............

"Come on Clarkey, you prat, into the kitchen and you can make us all a pot of coffee and by the way we've had to put you both in a twin room if that's ok?" I felt someone's

Dunge Bottom

blue/grey eyes burning into the back of my head as I quickly scurried away to make the coffee whilst Len and Bobbie acquainted themselves with PJ. Luckily she found the whole thing amusing and assured me she would be safe in a single bed in the twin room even if I was in the next bed.

The rest of the evening was a blur until we eventually were shown to our room by some of Len and Bobbies' younger children. At last, thought I, time to recommence the wooing.

The room was beautifully decorated and furnished in the Rococo period and had magnificent views over the Orangery and formal gardens beyond. We undressed a little hesitantly apart from me who I must admit tend to rush things a bit so was in my single bed first, in order to watch PJ prepare for her slumbersUnfortunately I was somewhat distracted to note that the bed not only had a Mister Men Duvet cover on it as did PJ's but the under sheet was plastic, in order as I was later to learn, to protect from urinary incontinence. PJ was reassured to learn that as a result, that my ardour was delightfully dampened. I was clinging to the hope that there might still be a window of opportunity in the morning; dream on Johnny. I spent a restless night as it was unseasonably warm and therefore sweaty and I had difficulty in maintaining position on the plastic sheets. At about six, we were awoken not by the expected trilling of the dawn chorus, as the mountain Choughs circled slowly over the dale but by four small children all under six charging into our room to give us Lupin injections of all things. I think they meant Lupus and I don'know where they got the idea from but at that time in the morning I cared very little. "Ah well back to the drawing board", this wooing business was much more difficult than it seemed at first glance.

One of my most endearing traits I am told is annoying persistence. I used it to its full potential by pursuing PJ over time until grudgingly and with scarcely disguised incredulity she agreed to marry me. I found out later that her capitulation was entirely due to my father's shoes.

A Busy Saturday Morning

I must mention the night before PJ and I married............

You see I couldn't go on a stag night as:

a. I had no friends and

b. I had to complete my VAT return.

So after completing the said VAT return I decided to double check all the travel documents, i.e., passports, driving licenses, rail tickets for the train on which we were to travel to Venice. All in order then, except my passport which had already expired!

"Oh Bugger, Oh God, Oh Save Me..." There was I getting married the very next morning staying over at the Brook House hotel on the Saturday night, leaving early on Sunday morning to travel down to London St. Pancras and onwards on our honeymoon, except of course we weren't as I had no passport. I do remember mentioning to my parents at the moment of discovery that one day I would look back at this time and laugh.

I am still waiting for that moment.

The morning of my marriage arrived and before meeting my beloved at the church I just needed to meet with our solicitor to sign the contract to buy our first house and try and get a twelve month visitor's passport from the post office. All went swimmingly well. Dressed in my wide lapelled flared dapper aubergine suit, covered fortunately

Dunge Bottom

by an old grubby grey brown mackintosh I visited down town Burton on Trent. All went very well, except I couldn't make the solicitor hear me knocking at their office door, so I couldn't sign the contract to buy our house and it was a complete disaster at the Post Office. There I was standing in a queue at the main Post Office in New Street, Burton, disguised by my grubby mac clutching, talisman like, my birth certificate and application forms for a twelve month visitor's passport.

Eventually my turn arrived at the counter, I handed over my forms and cheque and waited breathlessly for the issue of my passport. I waited a while, then waited again until I heard the encouraging voice behind the counter say....

"Sorry but we don't issue Visitors passports on a Saturday"

"What" said I this cannot be true "don't you realize I am getting married in two hours to the most wonderful woman in the world who when realizing that we cannot go on our once in a lifetime honeymoon will never ever forgive me"

"I'm very sorry but we don't issue passports on a Saturday" said the voice from hell. At this point I developed a cunning plan. Immediately I dropped to my knees in the middle of the large Post Office waiting hall, in front of a large assembled crowd and burst into tears. At hearing my predicament the whole of the waiting throng of customers immediately clamoured loudly in my support, demanding help from the faceless official behind the counter. I have only ever been so low twice in my life and I now know God does exist as the faceless official relented and ushered me into an interview room where they issued my passport.

I do not unfortunately know that person's name but I will be forever grateful to them for saving my marriage.

So on to the church...

By the way I just thought to mention at this point that I didn't actually attend the service wearing a dirty old mac and a wide lapelled flared aubergine suit. Even I don't live that near the edge!!

A Train and Teeth

I had decided that PJ the memsahib deserved the most romantic honeymoon that I could think of. I had by now developed an inclination towards the New Romantic scene, so needed to think of something really special. Well I had already tried Cromer, so that is right out. What to do? I have it! A three week honeymoon in Italy, travelling by the Orient Express to Venice, staying there for a few days then spend the rest of the time generally touring that most beautiful of countries.

After the wedding we retired to our hotel in Rollestonon-Dove, but unfortunately had to be up very early next morning to take a taxi to Snow Hill Station in Birmingham to catch the train to London so we could join the Orient Express. This meant we couldn't enjoy the all inclusive full English breakfast that I had particularly looked forward to, as well as married life of course m'dear.

Am I alone in hating Coventry? You see we were traveling on a Sunday by British Rail, which is just the day when they practise repairing the tracks or signalling gubbins or some such rubbish. Our time table was fairly tight anyway so to sit outside Coventry station for an hour waiting for the signalmen to finish their meal break was a wait too far. They did later deny that it was a meal break when I questioned them searchingly by letter. Stress levels were rising visibly although the Memsahib stayed remarkably calm as she was unaware of the exact timings. In fact I have come to learn that time and PJ., do not readily co exist. She, bless her, works in a completely different space time continuum.

Trying to plan catching flights and ferries has since always proven problematical, as she is completely oblivious to real earth time, so making leaving the house in time to catch something turns into a game of bluff and double bluff with an occasional triple bluff thrown in. We once planned to holiday with our friends The Terrific Turners, whom we were to meet at a southern ferry port, where we were to go over as foot passengers to France. Oddly enough we left late, actually very late even for us, travelled down in torrential driving rain and having to use speeds that one only sees in a car chase movie. As we pulled into the ferry port we could see our ferry, closing the bow doors. "Shit we've missed it" I explained to PJ. All we could do was to screech to a halt outside the terminal offices, grab our suitcases, throw the keys towards the bemused staff member, shouting park the car please we'll be back in a fortnight. We ran full pelt across the quayside as the gang plank was being hauled away from the side of the ship. "Shit we've missed it" I explained again to PJ. But the kindness of the crew saved the day as they saw our plight and heard our heavy breathing and lowered it again so we could join our chums. I'm so terribly sorry I really don't know why I had to relate that incident as it absolutely nothing to do with this bit, please forgive whilst I return to the story. As luck would have it we did make the connection and joined the Orient Express about ten minutes before it was due to leave.

It was a real eye opener, the ambiance, service, food and wine were extraordinary. In fact I have longed to dine somewhere where you choose the food to go with the wine – magnificent. We travelled at a regal pace down towards Folkestone, where we were to join a cross channel ferry.

John Clarke

The ambiance, service, food etc. were so good I was feeling more than a little tipsy by the time we reached Biggin Hill. It was a sensuous superior feeling being escorted from the train of trains and onto the ferry, passing the hoi polloi queuing up in their cars and cattle trucks – wow how the other half live, I could get used to this. Luckily the hurricane force wind that besieged the channel the day before and subsided to a storm force ten gale which meant that the ferries were actually able to sail today. I use the word luck in its broadest possible sense as I found out that I am not the best of sailors. You meet the nicest of people vomiting over the side of a ferry. Over the next hour or so, which I can assure you felt much longer, I struck up an intermittent conversation with the Orient Express piano player who was to travel with us to Venice. So much so when we entered the dining car for our pre dinner drinks he seamlessly switched tunes into "As time Goes By", our tune. Mucho brownie points there me thinks. Our main gourmet adventure was to have that romantic candle lit supper whilst standing in the Gare Du Nord station in Paris. By that I mean the Orient Express was standing in the station not us. I don't want anyone to think that I was being a cheap skate. The whole atmosphere was magical. I'm sure you've seen the old black and white films and can picture the scene where steam rises sensually against the sides of the train, the light from the windows glistens like diamonds on the wet platform and there are wistful stares from the poor people staring up at the hero and heroine dining in outrageous opulence. Actually one of those poor people looks ominously familiar. I cleared away the condensation from our window and see, with his nose pressed firmly up against the glass, Roger, our best man and hang gliding club embroiderer,

Dunge Bottom

who has followed us to Paris. Recognition lights his face
and he smiles..................
Oh no those teeth, Argh!!.

10

Gliding and Looping the Loop

I found, following my microlight accident, that due to a paralysed right arm and broken back, working was even now not a real possibility. So for about an eighteen month period I needed to keep myself amused. What could I do, one armed? The answer seemed obvious, I would learn to fly gliders, only this time the full sized ones with huge long wings and no engines that are either towed up into the air by means of a long rope and a winch or dragged up behind a tug aeroplane. So my chum Mr. Turner introduced me to the Marchington Gliding Club, who not only offered trial flights but also taught people to fly.

There were two main groups at the club, the weekend fliers and the Wednesday club and it was the latter that I chose to fly with as it was this one that Mr Turner visited most often and so I was able to cadge a lift. I spent many sessions there slowly learning the extra skills needed to

Dunge Bottom

fly one of these huge gliders. When I say huge the wing span was about fifty feet whilst my hang glider was only about thirty feet tip to tip. The big gliders used for training were a mixture of wood and fabric, not terribly safe if they crashed but then that was not the object. Some were made of fibreglass and others metal, both of which were slightly more reassuring. The thing that they all had in common was that they were two seaters. Normally the instructor sat behind the student because, as they used to say, they were further away from the crash.

The Wednesday Club were a very kind group of mainly retired folks or shift workers and the whole atmosphere was much more relaxed than the seemingly more pressurized week end crowd. They were so lovely and helpful in fact that in the early days of my recovery from the injuries when I couldn't move much without being in extreme pain they used to physically lift me up and sit me in the glider whilst firmly strapping me in.

At that time I had fitted a metal contraption which I fondly referred to as my claw. The paralysis in my arm meant that I could grip things normally but once having done so I couldn't extend my fingers to let go. So PJ fitted me out with a brace that went over my forearm and had metal wires extending over the back of all my fingers at the end of which were leather loops. These fitted over my finger ends which because of the spring in the metal kept my fingers straight. I could of course use my normal muscles to grip things and the spring effect of the claw meant I could then let go again. On the back of the claw where the metal wires met was a circular metal coil which gave the springiness and was just big enough to fit over the control stick of the glider. So I could hook myself up and fly my craft by moving my shoulder and upper arm about. All the instructors, when first introduced to me and my special equipment, were initially horrified until they saw that I could actually fly the thing at which point they gradually began to relax.

One of the criteria for flying the gliders was that if you hadn't flown for a month or so you needed a check ride in a two seat glider complete with instructor to make sure you could remember which way was up and generally still fly safely. So it came to pass that such a day arrived when I needed one of the check flights. With the normal assistance from my ground crew I duly found myself in the front of a two seat all metal Blanik glider (the most reassuring type) with Ron, my check flight instructor, in the back. Ron was a cheerful electronics engineer from Lichfield who always flew with the Wednesday crowd and just loved flying. It was Ron who had been instrumental in me getting my solo licence.

"Right" said Ron, "I just want a safe clean take off, a nice fly around with a good circuit prior to a smooth landing. Looking at the sky, I expect it will be a bit bouncy and should prove good fun. You have control"

So early afternoon on that April Wednesday, I gave the hand signal to start the flight and slowly oh slowly we began to accelerate down the bumpy grass runway, behind the trusty tug aircraft. Ron was right about the conditions because trying to stay behind and in line with the tug was proving difficult. The tug was about two hundred feet in front of us, so if he hit a bubble of rising air he would shoot upwards leaving us far below and subsequently when the tug had flown through the thermal lift and hit the descending air the other side we were just entering the lift that he had left, if you follow. This meant that the situation was reversed and we were now high above the much lower tug aircraft, fun indeed. I was a bit too busy trying to keep position to look out over the expanding patchwork of fields down below or, in fact, enjoy the flight much at all. At two thousand feet we cut away from the tow rope and watched as the tug aircraft lazily turned onto its side and descended back towards the airfield for its next customer.

The spring sunshine was surprisingly hot, you could feel it through the Plexiglas cockpit cover, but the north westerly wind was still cold, and as a result the thermals were very powerful due to the big difference in relative temperatures; so much so that we were easily able to climb to four thousand feet in the bouncing boisterous air. It was a truly magical feeling entering this huge bubble of invisible lift, feeling the initial turbulence then, by standing the glider on its wingtip and turning sharply, you could continuously climb two or three thousand feet until you reached the misty moisty dark grey sanctuary that was cloud base. No power and all for free. After the hard work of being towed by the tug plane, I was really enjoying myself. This is, without doubt, my favourite kind of flying.

It was a classic day and we had great fun. After about half an hour Ron said it was time to land and let someone else have a go. This was disappointing. It had been a long winter without any decent gliding and this was my first trip of the year. I was loving every moment of the strong lift and rapid climbs to cloud base. The last thing I wanted to do was go and land. A thought then occurred to me as the all metal glider we were flying was certified for aerobatics. I excitedly asked Ron.

"Is there any chance of doing some aerobatics? It's a great chance to learn some and of course we'll lose height quicker." I was hoping he would he would fall for my ploy.

John Clarke

"Good idea" he ventured, "have you done any loops yet?"

"No in fact I haven't done any aeros yet", I responded eagerly

"Ok, how about a loop" said Ron,

"Great", I muttered and swallowed nervously.

"OK, it's easy", he reassured me, "Just push the nose down and speed up to about ninety knots, pause, then pull the stick back fully, look back and wait for the horizon to appear then keep going around until the world is the right way up again."

"Easy Peasy" I thought. "Okay, here goes." I took a deep breath, checked the altimeter which showed four thousand feet, narrowed my eyes against the steady drip of nervous sweat that suddenly formed on my brow and hoped.

Well the ninety knots bit went well, although we did seem to be diving down very steeply with the ground rushing up towards us very quickly indeed, despite it being over three thousand feet away. It was an assault on the senses with the soundtrack of an ever increasing rushing noise of the air blasting past the cockpit canopy. The pressure on the control stick was becoming much firmer. I pulled back on the stick and the aircraft responded. I felt an enormous pressure forcing me back into the seat so much so that it seemed difficult to breathe normally. As the glider climbed vertically, all I could see was the blue sky and the towering cumulus clouds. The noise of the wind died as quickly as it had built up. Slowly, and ever so gently, the nose of the glider went past the vertical and we were completely upside down. I looked back, as instructed, it was now simply a matter of waiting for the ground to come into view.

Except it didn't.

The bloody glider just stopped upside down and stayed

there! There was none of the expected nose carrying on over until it dropped and pointed earthwards. We had just stopped completely upside down. Incidentally, I never realised how much dust and muck hides in the floor of a glider. It rained down on both of us causing not some little distress. Ron's voice cut through my confusion. "Oh that's where my pen went". After what seemed quite a significant amount of time, I asked Ron what he thought I should do now as I was sure that we really weren't supposed to be stopped upside down. "Buggered if I know", was the encouraging response.

"Interesting, but a little unhelpful" I thought. At that moment the glider decided to carry on as normal. The nose dropped as originally expected and we were now diving straight down towards the ground "Shit" I probably announced to any interested listener as we were diving down vertically towards the earth at what seemed like warp speed with the wind noise now deafening and the control stick increasingly hard to move.

"Pull up Clarkey" said Ron, with just a hint if urgency in his scream. I pulled harder than I have ever pulled before on the control stick. It felt like all my internal organs would appear naked for the entire world to see as they exited my body via my rectum. As if that wasn't enough the G forces were trying to force me out through the floor of the glider. I quickly resumed straight and level flight and commenced breathing normally again.

Silence reigned for a brief period whilst Ron and I mentally digested our recent experience and tried to make sense of what had happened.

"That was odd" I muttered glancing at the altimeter which now showed four thousand three hundred feet.

"Bloody hell Ron we're higher now than when we

started. Let's do some more." Ron very quietly suggested that we pop out the airbrakes and gently descend back to the airfield.

"Aw come on Ron that was great let's do some more." I repeated having now recovered some composure and experienced a returning sense of adventure.

"Land the bloody glider" said Ron with an unusual degree of steely emphasis and, I dare say, determination. "Are you sure, couldn't we just do another one now I've got the hang of it?" I enquired innocently.

"Land the bleedin' glider!"

I landed the glider.

During the debrief the colour returned to Rons cheeks and after several cups of hot sweet tea so did his composure and sense of humour. "Did I pass okay Ron and when can you and I go and do some more aerobatics" I enquired enthusiastically.

"Yes you passed the check flight fine, but I think we'll miss out on the aeros for a little while" was all he said, in a tone that brooked no questioning.

"Perhaps someone else will let me do some more" I thought as I waddled off towards the canteen. "Someone who hasn't spoken to Ron". The canteen was located in a coach where you could enjoy one of Iris's all day breakfasts. I was hoping to share the tale of my latest gliding exploit with anyone who would care to listen. I wondered if I could find anyone to come with me again. Since I was now sure I could fly one upside down next time. We later worked out that as the nose of the glider went over we entered the centre of a really strong thermal. This stopped the glider from completing its rotation over the top of the circle, so that we were actually climbing in the rising air whilst being upside down! I do suspect that this stopping upside down is quite a rare event and in fact I've yet to hear of anyone sharing the same experience.

One of the most exciting bits about my glider flying, was learning to how to thermal fly with an experienced instructor behind me. My previous hang gliding attempts had been less successful as I was trying to work it all out on my own. Once I had learnt some of the thermalling tricks I was always keen when solo flying to nip off somewhere miles away and find my way back to the airfield. Regretfully I was not as successful at this as I would have liked usually ending up hopelessly lost. This I think is a genetic fault with me as I seem to get lost whenever and wherever I go. As the following chapter, while not actually flying related, shows.

11

"Well It Was There Yesterday!"

In a former life I happened to be involved in a property
company, when in the good times and, yes, there were
some then, not like nowadays, we decided we needed to
buy a company boat, so...

We ended up meeting an amazing man, Dave, who lived
on the Hamble (well obviously not on the Hamble which is
a river, although technically he could have lived on a boat,
although he didn't he lived with his wife and lads in a house
near the Hamble – I do sometimes wonder if in my quest for
accuracy I lose the flow a little. Dave was a designer and
boat builder. In fact we ended up sailing one of his motor
sailors, A Profile 42, which was a fabulous motor sailor type
boat, built out of concrete, fitted out beautifully in teak and
other exotic hardwoods.

Thinking on however, I did at the time and probably still
do wonder how on earth something forty two foot long and
made of concrete could actually float, but I can assure you

that it certainly did, which was fortunate. Dave was a real craftsman, who can actually make wood go around corners. You see the inside of his boat was all curves and to fit it out so well was a real work of art.

He helped us to buy the company boat, which was a twenty nine foot power boat, sleeping four with two one hundred and thirty horse power Volvo Penta petrol engines which on a good day could propel it to fifty knots or so; which is really quick apparently.

It also had been or indeed still was the fastest boat on the Solent.

Anyway one night we were all gathered at Dave & Sue's house enjoying one or two Pimms when he suggested that it would be a good idea for us to gain experience and do a night crossing over to the Isle Wight and visit a particular pub in Ventnor which he rated very highly for its selection of Malts. After the fourth bottle of wine we had hatched a plan.

We would meet at the Slightly Drunken Sailor pub at lunch time, compare tidal charts and times, enjoy one or two drinks then take the boat over at full tide, to make Ventnor with a view to either staying the night in the harbour or returning back to the Hamble and sleeping on the boat. Bright and early the next morning the intrepid adventurers met at the Slightly Drunken

Sailor, at about 1-00pm.

Our party consisted of me, another John and a Ray who were both compadres of the property group. Dave was supposed to be with us but had to cry off. He did however call and give us directions, saying, "You'll have no problems, just go into the Solent turn left a bit and Ventnor will be on your right hand side about one hour away." That was most encouraging as he was very much our naval mentor.

John Clarke

For the next three or four hours we pored over tidal charts, and wine lists. We unanimously decided to stock up on extra booze as we had learnt that alcohol and sailing go very much hand in hand. I am not sure if that is the current politically correct thinking nowadays but back in the seventies it was compulsory! Anyway, we slipped our berth (I thought that I would introduce a real naval term here just to show how much sailing jargon we had absorbed,) just as it was getting dark. Ray was at the helm, as we headed down the Hamble into the wild waters of the Solent, heading slightly left as instructed.

Things were going swimmingly well, so much so we thought that we would break out a particularly good bottle or two of Malt. We were very safety conscious as John and I would have doubles but Ray who was still at the helm and navigating would stick to singles. It was a very good bottle of Glenmorangie, so good in fact that we had to open another, Highland Park this time. It was a gentle relaxing time what with the soporific rocking of the boat and a gentle thrumming of the mighty Volvo Pentas beneath our feet. We were so soporific in fact we both fell asleep confident in the dedication of our helmsman, idiots that we were.

Why on earth did we believe that Ray could be relied upon? After some little while, I was awoken by a heavy thumping noise from above followed by muttered cursing. "What to do eh?" I thought I had better go and investigate. I poked the other John in the ribs, which elicited a large farting noise followed by grunting. Whereupon we ventured up top only to find that Ray had stopped swearing and had now stood up having apparently fallen asleep at the wheel and ended up on the deck.

Suddenly nothing happened.

Dunge Bottom

There was an almost full moon, which cast a soft light over the scene. An eerie phosphorescence lit the sea very much like it is in the South China Seas, all that was missing was the sight of blue whales gorging on the plankton. We all looked around in silence and awe noticing that apart from the aforementioned it was very dark. It was very dark indeed. "Hang on a minute" we thought, "dark? It can't be dark I mean the Isle of Wight has got lots of lights on it, hasn't it?" In fact it remained very dark, apart from a block of lights behind us and to our right. Relief flooded through the boat, "Ventnor at last" seems a bit off course mind you but no matter, so we gently turned the boat around towards the lights. Shouldn't be long now thinks us all, and a good job too, we were running out of booze, time critical indeed. After a short while, Ray the ever observant helmsman asked for confirmation that Ventnor was moving?

We looked and were glad to confirm that it was indeed moving. Now after some little while we realized that Ventnor shouldn't move, nor should it look like a Brittany Ferries Cruise ferry, which it appeared to be turning out to be. "Bloody hell!" we all said it perfect unison. "Where the hell are we?" we again said together. At this point we decided that a working supper type conference was needed to resolve this particularly thorny problem. It lasted about one minute, as the other John, always a leader and decision maker, immediately barked out the order to Ray, who was being made to feel responsible for our present predicament "Follow that ferry!" We would at least arrive at land sometime soon as ferries start and stop at the hard bits after all.

After a brief time, Ray who was now trying to assert himself again, and returning to the task of steering our little ship, pointed out that we were now according to the compass heading South by South West. We internalized this bit of technical information, chewed it over and re internalized again only to consider that it would appear that we were going the wrong way, towards France. In fact as I already had great experiences with car ferries due to my extended travels abroad especially to the near continent I was confident that we were heading towards Caen Ouistreham, which is an attractive little port and seaside town and near where some of the British troops landed on D Day. I was about to embark on a sort of historical information session with my chums when I was interrupted by both of them uttering, "Heck, what do we do now?" I was able to reassure them that although we could at this point in time consider ourselves to be in dire straits, we should fear not as I had learnt a navigational trick from an RAF Flying Instructor friend of mine, namely...

Whilst taking out a brand new student pilot in a Jet Provost military trainer on a first time navigational exercise, he noted that the tyro pilot was becoming increasing pale and sweaty, as the ground whistled past at about four miles a minute, and as the new bod was becoming more and more lost. My chum the instructor just sat there and said nothing until eventually the student pilot threw up his hands in sheer panic....

"Sorry sir but we are lost and gone, I've absolutely no idea where we are", are he spurted out. My mate just said,

"So we're lost then are we?"

"Yes sir, hopelessly"

"Lets see if we can sort things out then, What hemisphere are we in?"

"Northern, sir"

"Good, what country?"

"England"

Dunge Bottom

"Very good m'boy, have a guess at a county"
A slight hesitation followed by "Derbyshire?"

"Excellent, so we are somewhere in Derbyshire then, look out of the window and what can you see?"
"A big lake sir."
"What shape is it, and compare it with the map you've got on your knee"
A short pause followed by...........
"Derwent Reservoir?"
"Brilliant so we were never lost at all then were we?"
"No sir."
This was a salutary lesson for us all I suspect. So I immediately called upon the above to assert my own leadership status and save the situation..."Turn round and steer in exactly the opposite direction" I barked out and quickly.

"Thank God we're saved" came the cry. At least now we know that we are heading back towards England somewhere, although exactly how far to go was a bit of a worry. You see there was no such thing as GPS in those days. We also were concerned as to both the fuel and alcohol levels as we suspected both were possibly becoming increasingly critical. All we could do was to hang on and hope for the best.

After a couple of hours of nerve racking tension, imagining that the mighty thrumming from the Volvo Pentas was becoming slightly less steady due to shortage of fuel, we began to see what we hoped was a faint line of lights directly ahead of us. We were saved!

Another hour passed worryingly by and we now noticed that there were lights to our left, followed by a black bit in front and lights again to our right. Again following my RAF

John Clarke

chum as before described, we surmised correctly and surprisingly for us with our track record, that we were entering the Solent, with the Isle of Wight on our left and with the mouth of the Hamble and home fast approaching on our right. It was next lunchtime, in the Slightly Drunken Sailor, when we rather sheepishly regaled Dave, our sailing chum, with the details of our night's adventure.

I must admit that he was perhaps fair to say that our antics called into question the law that allowed bumbling amateurs to go out and play with boats in the oceans, and put at risk the lives of the emergency services who had to go and rescue cretins like us........and as Dave pointed out with incredulity,

"For Pete's sake how could you miss the Isle of Wight?" At this point we all felt that we in for an extended lecture and we were saved by Ray, bursting out, with righteous indignation and blistering accuracy??............

"Well it was there yesterday!"

12

Pink Floyd and Larimore

Back to flying. Now previously I mentioned my chum Turner. Now Mr Turner likes to think outside the box, especially with his family and pets. In fact I was very fortunate to know Pink Floyd before they were famous. Actually, I am not sure if I am misleading you a little here, unintentionally of course. It isn't Pink Floyd the band, oh no! It's an Alsatian dog, with a little bit of collie thrown in for good measure. He was named Pink Floyd by Kate, Mr. Turners daughter. She shared many of her father's interests as she too rode motorbikes and wore leathers. Kate couldn't help but notice that Floyd, as was his given name, had a propensity for licking his own tadger and he being a large manly sort of a dog, had one that was difficult to avoid seeing.

Hence the name of Pink Floyd.

PF, as I will now affectionately call him, was fed and watered by Turner. I refrain from stating that he was owned by Turner as PF could never be owned by any human being. Now Turner, is an interesting man. I met him via hang gliding as he came to me to learn how to fly. He was and still is, an accomplished pilot of gliders, and powered aircraft. A hobby he paid for by working on the oil rigs on a two week on and two week off rota. So he had plenty of time and money to play and to buy toys, like gliders and motorbikes and go flying! One of the more expensive toys was his Breitling watch that I was very much envious of, a Chronograph Navitimer to be precise. One day I hope to be able to afford a replica of such a thing. We gelled almost immediately sharing the same sense of humour, similar rants about what was wrong with the world and most importantly our love of all things aviation. He had some of the attributes of Victor Meldrew and delighted in gently winding people up. We have been mates ever since In fact it was Turner who got me into fixed wing gliding by joining the Wednesday Club at Marchington.

PF also loved going there with his human because I suspect that he not only enjoyed running around chasing rabbits, but it was there that he, in his own doggy style (no pun intended) fell in love!

With Larimore.

How to describe Larimore? Another of my gliding chums. His appearance was always just on the edge of scruffy and his dress code was at least a decade behind the times. This at a time when even up to date fashion was somewhat dubious. He was chubby, with intimidating jowls that distracted you when he talked. As well as pursuing his flying hobbies, Larimore helped with the hang gliding training and worked for Rolls Royce in Derby. For someone who might be described as a practical man, even a 'manly' man you always knew when he was coming. He had an inexhaustible supply of the strongest smelling cheap after- shave imaginable. When he visited he would settle comfortably in a chair, usually with a glass of whisky in his hand and wobetide the host who did not supply him with one. The ultimate compliment to the persons he was gracing with his visit was that he would then go on to remove his shoes. Any remnant of the gentle nose of the Glenmorangie would be immediately replaced by Old Spice and slightly sweaty Lenor. I don't know why I didn't just serve him Kwik Save Scotch and have done with it.

So one afternoon Larimore arrived at the gliding club. He mounted the steps of the old coach which serves as the club house and canteen with the intention of enjoying one of Iris's famous all day cooked breakfasts. Iris's breakfasts were so delicious we used to have the police round regularly when they were in the area to enjoy one of her specials. Anyway, Larimore came into the coach, sat down and started chatting away innocently enough. He started to become slightly uncomfortable when PF sat next to him staring fixedly straight into his eyes. Larimore was a friendly sort where animals were concerned and patted the dog on the head. This was a grave mistake. Before he could take his hand away PF turned towards Larimore, clasped his front paws around him, and started to hump his left arm.

Now this was not some little Yorkshire Terrier, embarrassing, inconvenient but ultimately harmless. PF was a big dog, in every sense, and this event was not something that Larimore could shrug off easily. It was also extremely, startlingly obvious to all sitting in the coach. Silence fell as this act unfolded, Larimore bravely tried to continue the conversation while becoming more and more uncomfortable, especially as the giggling started. We all know how infectious giggling is and when Turner starts it is even more difficult not to join in. Apart from Larimore of course who was getting the rogering of a lifetime and having tried it now decided that enough was enough.

"Get this bloody dog off me!" he calls out.

More giggling.

"For Christ's sake, Chas. get him off " At this point he was rescued by the pilot's call of "Glider downwind"

At this everyone, including PF, who considered this the only thing more important than sexual gratification using strangers' limbs, left the coach and started to walk towards the runway. The call meant that there was a glider about to land and they would need help to push it off the runway and back towards the launch area. This was important, as without it, the runway would become clogged up with gliders and additionally we would also run out of aircraft, as they were all parked on the runway. It was ground control at its most basic.

This, then, was the saving of Larimore as PF left off his amorous doings to join all on the runway. (He also enjoyed chasing after the gliders as they were much easier to catch than the rabbits, they didn't disappear down holes. Ten of us marched over the runway in a loose 'V' formation when I heard Turner very quietly mutter;

"Go get him, Floyd" shortly followed by a desperate cry.

"Oh for God's sake he's doing it again".

This strangled cry came from Larimore who we noticed now had PF firmly clamped onto his right leg, humping away with even more vigour, as Larimore struggled to keep up with the group. We all had difficulty pretending not to have heard Larimore's increasingly desperate cries and Turner had even taken the opportunity to go and start up the tug aircraft ready for the next launch.

Now, no one else had the bravery, or foolishness to go

to assist Larimore. PF was a big dog and was in love. No one in their right mind would want to interfere, and we needed to let nature take its course. After all not even PF could go on forever.

Mind you, he did try, and I think it had a considerable influence on Larimore's decision not to attend the Wednesday Club in future.

I said earlier that PF was thrilled by the journey to the gliding club. This was I suspect due to being force fed all the delightful smells of the surrounding countryside on his journey from Derby to Marchington. By this I mean that Turner enjoyed his motorbikes. He had a fair collection, and he used to like to come over to the club on his BMW K100RS Sports Tourer. Now, PF could not ride pillion but Turner had a wheeze. He stuffed PF in a large rucksack with just his head sticking out and slung it over his back. So, at mostly illegal road speeds, PF would have his ears streaming back in the wind, nostrils fully opened and eyes as big as saucers, overdosing on the scents of the countryside. Unfortunately PF found this type of travel, although rewarding and exciting did have a large disadvantage in that his eyes became filled with dust and grit. To counter this most dog lovers would have reverted back to travelling by car...not so Turner. Mark IV flying goggles, that was the answer. These were the sort that had two separate eye pieces and an elasticated head band.

Imagine.

You see a blur as a huge silver BMW motorbike arrives at the airfield at high speed, ridden by a suspicious figure swathed in black leather with a dog, wearing flying goggles, ears streaming back in the wind, peering anxiously over Turner's shoulders desperately looking out for the true love of his life, Larimore!

Dunge Bottom

PF wasn't just a land based extreme sports dog, he loved hang gliding as well. He couldn't actually control the glider of course, he was dog. But he loved being there watching his human. "Can you make me a harness for PF?" asked Turner one day whilst lying on the grass at Edge Top near Longnor waiting for the wind to change. Wind conditions were always a problem, for no matter which site you went to the wind conditions were never absolutely right. In fact we spent most of our flying lives driving to and from the flying sites and waiting for the conditions to change. Usually the wind was either too light, so we would end up flying to the bottom with the inevitable hell of carrying back up again, or too strong with the dangers of being blown back over the top of the hill, and being dumped unceremoniously, often painfully, in the turbulent rotored air, or, more rarely, waiting for it to blow up the face of the hill so we could take off at all.

"Sorry Chas, what did you say?" I grant you it wasn't much of a conversation but I was snoozing at the time and having an interesting dream about chocolate eclairs.

"Can you make a harness for Floyd, so I can take him up with me?" he repeated.

It was an odd request and to be honest I thought nothing more of it, until unexpectedly, Turner arrived with PF for an official measuring.

After some while we decided PF would be excited (in that special doggy way) about actually leaving the ground, so I would have to make allowances in a certain part of the harness to allow for this. A few stitches, some old strapping and it was completed.

The time had come for a test flight.

Again Edge Top was the chosen venue, mainly because you could park right at the top not more than ten yards

John Clarke

away from the launch point. I had really got the no walking anywhere policy down to a T. Gliders were rigged and Turner fitted the harness on Pink Floyd, who it had to be said looked somewhat bemused by the process, but nonetheless stood there whilst he was clipped into the glider and, this done, Turner launched off into the turbulent air. He climbed in the slope lift to about a hundred feet above the top and flew backwards and forwards across the face of the hill. "How is it?" I called up to them. Obviously at this point I was expecting Turner to reply, but I swear PF, turned round, looked over Turner's shoulder, straight down at me, ears streaming in the wind, flying goggles on, and grinned. It may have been the wind in my eyes. I did also get a reply from Turner saying PF seemed to be enjoying this flying lark and that we would need to make alterations to the harness to allow for expansion!

From that day on, whenever Turner arrived to fly PF would sniff about in Turner's kitbag, find his own harness and follow Turner around the site with it trailing from his mouth. A doggy success I suspect.

Whilst recounting tales of Mr. Turner I cannot leave him without making mention of what is perhaps his greatest achievement in his long and distinguished existence on this planet. He is a truly remarkable wordsmith. Not quite as elevated as Shakespeare or Chaucer, not quite an equal with Mr. Oxford or indeed the contemporary and popular Mr Fry. For these great wordsmiths encompassed the mighty breadth of the English language and as a result it can perhaps be fairly said that they never quite mastered it completely. Mr Turner however was a true to the wordsmith ethos. He specialised in just one word.

Mr. Turner, now retired, is intelligent in many ways, gifted practically, a great flyer, I do believe as I mentioned before that the character of Victor Meldrew was modelled on Mr. T. But most important of all he specialises in Bastard. Now the English language is very special and has subtleties foreigners can only dream of. It is an immense language which if allowed could intimidate all who try and master it. Not so Turner. He very cleverly decided that his life's work should be to master a specific part of our wonderous tongue. To be specific that one word.

Bastard.!!

To try I explain how he did it I will need to try and spell the word phonetically, thus avoiding problems with the subtle nuances of pronunciation of this important word. Here goes. The normal person in the street would say BASS TADD. This is a very thin pronunciation and can be heard extensively in general conversation particularly amongst the Jeremy Kyle generations who struggle with the delicacies of our mother tongue. It is offensive, entirely negative and can and often does lead to traumatic injuries. By far a better way of pronunciation, is, dare I suggest,

BARRS TUD.

Try the difference for yourselves dear reader. The change of spelling turns a crass, offensive utterance into one that can be used in front of Royalty and indeed by them. It is a woody word that can be tuned to perfection by simply adding or removing the number of "R" s. Its use can now cover the whole range of our joyous language. Try it for yourselves, use it every day, try and include it more and more in general conversation. Let it become a favourite noun, revel in its majesty, cheer its consonants, rejoice in its vowels, savour its syllables. This is truly one of the greatest words in the English language. Become a disciple for its use; let its cry ring out far and wide throughout the land and pay homage to Mr. Turner for his great insight.

John Clarke

Rejoice, Dear Reader, Rejoice for now too, you have conquered our mother tongue.

13

Did We Beat The Bastards?

At one stage I was invited to be the "wind dummy" for the British Hang Gliding Team competing against the French at the annual Bleriot Cup.

Wind Dummy is not the most honourable of titles and, as you can imagine, is not the most honourable of roles. Essentially you are the sacrificial team member who is thrown off the hills or cliffs first, with hang glider attached of course, to test the conditions and see if it is safe for the rest of the team members to fly. Len, the second hand car salesman, was the team manager. He wanted a lift rather than using his own car and so kindly invited me to take this exalted position.

Now driver and wind dummy sounds unimpressive (and indeed it was) but I was keen due to one important reason. This was a famous international competition which was battled out in the full glare of the world's spotlight. Being against the French, it had the weight of history behind it and the rivalry was intense. The competition had been running since the early Nineteen Eighties, with the venue alternating between each country. As you might expect bitter rivalry between the two national teams was the order of the day, not just because of Agincourt and other such historical troubles but because the French had a reputation for cheating. At this point I do not wish to disparage the entire French nation by stating that they cheat at all sports (although they do) but this particular gliding team had what one would call a liberal interpretation of the rules. Also, this was the chance of an all expenses paid trip to the South of France with all the wine, exotic food, groupies and of course, flying that you could get.

"Any chance of travelling down with you?" asked Len when he first approached me with the offer.

"Yeh, no probs, but I'll need to renew my passport" I replied gleefully. I was by nature a very excitable and irritatingly keen kind of a person.

"Of course you will" grinned Len. I've made all the travel and accommodation arrangements, so there's nothing to worry about."

Boy was I excited. I mean not only flying with the British Team but flying on foreign shores, it didn't get any better than that. The mighty thermals of the Southern Pyrenees or the Alpes Maritimes during the long sunny days, the evenings basking in the glories and victories of the daily battles, nubile young French damsels hanging on my every word. Heaven. I could not wait for the day to arrive.

When at last the day to leave came I was up early and as I waited for Len I wondered how different it would be to be woken by the French Cockerel rather than my Tandy radio alarm clock. Len duly arrived and we loaded the car, lots of hang gliders on the roof, harness and bags in the boot. Sun cream oil and Raybans at the ready and I made sure I left some space for the duty free vino.

"Dover here we come" I yelled in eager anticipation as my Ford Granada surged forward

"Where?" questioned Len.

"Dover" I repeat, "or is it Ramsgate?" I enquired. Perhaps we were travelling on the hovercraft from Ramsgate instead of the ferry from Dover to keep costs down a bit. "Very sensible" I thought. "No wonder Len is the Team Manager."

"Aberystwyth, you prat" Len stated baldly, his face indicating the dawning realization that he is about to spend the next two weeks with a blithering idiot, albeit one who was very excitable and keen.

"You mean we are going to compete against the best French pilots in an international competition; in" and I must admit here my voice broke somewhat. "In bloody Aberystwyth?"

"Yes" was the devastating reply.

The rest of our journey to West Wales was completed in total silence apart from the occasional utterances of,

"Bloody hell, Aberystwyth" This from me.

I feel at this stage I must apologise to you, my no doubt sensitive readers, for my outburst. I can only plead disappointment at not visiting the hot sun kissed mountains of the South of France, along with the wine, exotic food, groupies and fabulous flying. I had heard so many tales from other pilots who had flown down there about the incredibly powerful thermals that cast you skywards whether you wanted to go or not, the baking heat, flying for miles down the great long gorges high above the trees until eventually landing out somewhere in the wilds of the French countryside, exhausted but satiated by the intoxicating flying. But instead we were driving to the wet and windy slate quarries of Wales and, to coin my new term

Dunge Bottom

for it "Bloody Aberystwyth."

When we finally arrived in Aber, it was, of course, raining. In Wales the rain does not fall but instead seems to be an integral part of the air. The town reflected the greyness of the day, and my mood, with wet stone houses topped with black slate roofs stretching off in all directions as we drove sullenly through. My sombre countenance did improve though when we got to the Town Hall where they were holding a Civic Reception in our honour. We met all the important local people, Mayor, Council members, Welsh Tourist Board officers. Also we had our first meeting with the not so important people, the French. So there we were in the Great Civic Chamber of the Town Hall, chatting over tea and cakes along with non alcoholic drinks, "bugger", and the interminable speeches in both English and Welsh, not French I was delighted to note, welcoming us all to this mighty festival of flight.

As for the French, they did, at least, begin to challenge my stereotypical ideas. They did not have long moustaches, they did not wear berets and they did not smell of onions. No, they all seemed of average height, coolly dressed, with an aloofness that only the French seem able to master and either being unable to or choosing not to speak any English. To say I had been disappointed about being in Aber., was nothing in comparison to how the French were feeling. Their disappointment was not only obvious by their surly looks out of the Town Hall windows into this grey world they had joined, but actually was most agreeable, to me at least. I didn't have chance at this point to compare thoughts with the rest of the team as I was being offered yet another water biscuit, which would have been churlish to refuse as it complimented my Orange Juice so well. I sat down on one of the chairs, before standing up again. I examined my squashed, and now unnecessary, Raybans and, with a long sigh, threw them in the bin.

The rest of the day was spent in settling in to our hotel, a large Victorian building right on the seafront. It was ageing but comfortable and warm with a bar that we were promised would stay open for as long as we liked. All our team assembled in the bar and started chatting about what was to come. Somehow things felt as if they were slowly getting better, especially after a few ginger wines. Besides our increasingly noisy selves, I could not help noticing a continuous background noise which filled the whole hotel. It could best be described as a low "twittering" sound, somewhat like an aviary full of budgies. It was difficult to place the source and eventually the whole of our team just stopped talking and listened attentively as we tried to track down its origin. We noted that we seemed to be sharing the hotel with a large number of mainly elderly ladies chasing their zimmer frames around albeit at very slow speed. On further careful examination we realized they were making the twittering noise we had been hearing. They were all twittering at the same time, either twittering to a specific individual or twittering to all, even sometimes to empty rooms and corridors. In case you aren't sure of what exactly a twitter is, I will define it for you.

The British Standard definition is basically the vocalisations of an elderly lady, mostly deaf, partially sighted, with a blue rinse, mobilising only with the assistance of a zimmer frame. We

watched in awe and couldn't help but notice that the twittering did seem to take the form of conversations, which initially were hard to follow. Typically a twitter went along the lines of...

"Who are all these young men, Margaret?"

Dunge Bottom

"What young men dear?"

"All those young men at the bar Margaret"

"What bar dear?, I really must try and find my spectacles"

Obviously now completely bored or distracted from this conversational thread, they continued.

"What colour did you have your hair done today Margaret?"

It was the day the visiting hairdresser came to the hotel, which explained the strange and vaguely unpleasant smell of setting solution that assailed our nostrils upon arrival.

"Whisper blue dear, what colour did you think it was?"

"Blue Margaret"

"Oh that's a relief dear, do you fancy a cup of tea?"

"Very nice dear"

All the time throughout this riveting conversation the two twitters in question were making very slow and unsteady progress towards the dining room where afternoon tea was being served. We carried on looking about us and realized that there were many simultaneous twitterings going on with such varied topics such as the weather, the food, sweets, television, the old days, young people, incontinence pants, filling the whole hotel with this white noise. We were here for two weeks. "Bloody hell."

Getting about the hotel's public rooms was also frustrating as no matter where you turned you encountered one of them, sometimes two, walking about on a random course, at very slow speed with the ability to cut off the overtaking lane seemingly with ease. Can you imagine the frustration of trying to get past a couple of them only to be thwarted and having as a consequence to endure listening to their twittering on and on about biscuits. Mind you after we got to know each other a little, they as a group were quite interested in why we young Bucks were there. Early

John Clarke

on in our stay I was approached by a lady, about four foot ten tall, with a pronounced curvature of the spine, very obvious arthritic hands, loosely fitting teeth and a blue rinse, who in a querulous voice announced,

"A competition you say dear"

I didn't but..."Yes a hang gliding competition with the French National Team"

"The French you say, I remember the Vichy French in the war, despicable people don't you know dear"

"Oh I don't know about that?"

"Where are the French people I don't seem to have seen any?"

"They are staying in another hotel, we will meet them tomorrow morning"

"Well I'm sure they are very nice dear. Hang gliding you say, what's that then?"

"We jump off hills on gliders and fly around, the winner is the one who stays in the air longest or flies the furthest.

"Sounds very dangerous dear, do you get killed often?"

"Just the once"

Usually the young buck has lost the will to live at this point and stands head bowed listening to the now one sided conversation disappearing off down the corridor. It would appear that none of our Twitters could understand the concept of a hang gliding competition, they could understand the concept of a French person, they could understand the concept of a competition, but no way could they understand anything about hang gliding. This was, after all, a new invention and as a result remained a complete mystery to most of them for the entire fortnight we were there. The only thing that they all agreed on was that we shouldn't have the bar open late into the night, certainly not past nine thirty anyway!

Dunge Bottom

Because the hotel was run at a speed the majority of the residents could handle our days naturally started gently enough with large English/Welsh breakfasts. I really enjoyed myself as I was the only there who would actually eat the bacon rinds, so I ended up with everyone's, "very nice dear". We then all watched the weather forecast on the television, followed by a team talk to discuss tactics for the day. The forecast led to one of two emotions. We were either disappointed due to unsuitable flying conditions. These happened a lot in Wales, so why the hell were here and not in France? A thought I would voice loudly to anyone who would care to listen. I was still bitter over the whole Aberystwyth situation. Alternatively we were excited because it looked as if we might get chance to fly. It surprised us how quickly the Twitters realised that the weather forecast was something very important to us. They had no actual understanding of why it was important, but none the less asked every morning if the weather was going to be "nice" for us. The word "nice" was heard ad nauseum throughout our stay there as it was the most common adjective used by the Twitters. The subject matter was irrelevant, someone could just have won the Euro Millions or been shat on by a manic elephant, the response would be exactly the same, "very nice dear."

Aberystwyth had been chosen because it was close to a huge number of flying sites, both inland and coastal. The locations also provided a feast of wind directions and, consequently, a range of challenges. Most of the competition tasks, stated in the most simplistic terms, required pilots to take off, fly around a bit and land as far away from the take off point as possible in the fastest possible time. This was all monitored by competition marshals who were scattered around the countryside in strategic positions to record the relevant times.

You may remember earlier my role was wind dummy, taking off first and testing the conditions before the rest of the team followed. I was also the British Team's secret weapon as I had reputation for extreme clumsiness. This was called on to good near the town of Machynlleth. Unfortunately no one could actually pronounce the name properly. To this day this small rural Welsh village is still referred to as Machinelathe amongst our group. We all set off to rendezvous at a lay by at the back of the hill that dominated the village. During the half hour drive excitement and tensions rose as we began psyching ourselves up for the task to come. Duly parked with our kit unloaded, we started to take the long hike along the track towards the take off area. It was really hard work as although still early in the morning the sun was making things uncomfortably warm. I know I have referred to a hill but it was actually a non picturesque old slate quarry, with a fifteen hundred feet sheer cliff face at the take off point. The top of the cliff was completely covered in various varieties of knee high sharp shrubbery and we were being attacked by enormous swarms of angry Welsh midgets, oops that should be midges, as we rigged the gliders. A more concerning problem was that there was no wind at all. Now normally no wind means that you have to run like a loony to generate enough speed for the glider to actually fly. For the glider to support both its own weight and the weight of the pilot it needs a certain speed of wind or air flowing over the sail to produce enough lift. In practical terms this usually means that you need about sixteen miles per hour over the sail. So in conditions where there is no wind it was down to me to prove that such flight was possible. I realized I would need to run through the knee high bracken at a minimum of sixteen miles per hour. Not an easy task, I can assure you. As you can see from some of the photographs I am unfortunately deformed, my legs are disproportionately short compared with my body and running like a loony does not come easy to me! As I contemplated my fate Len shouted at me to stop messing about and get off and check things out! I do a reccie and approach the edge of the cliff on hands and knees and peer over the edge of the abyss.

"OH CRAP"

I thought in capitals. I mean this is a fifteen hundred foot sheer drop after all! I could not put it off any longer and surrounded by a large group of pilots (at a respectful distance), I picked up the glider, which seemed twice the normal weight, took a few deep breaths, closed my eyes (old habits die hard) and commenced my charge towards the edge. All seemed to be going really well. I accelerated quickly and built up impressive speed. As I got near the edge I tripped over a particularly deep bit of bracken, fell over the edge and found myself pointing vertically down.

At this moment, somewhere in the deep dark recesses of my mind I heard a loud gasp of horror from the crowd, and as I feel myself going over the edge of the abyss, a spontaneous,

"By Gum!" escaped from my lips. I dared to open my eyes. The cliff face was blurred and passing directly underneath me at an increasingly high speed. I decided to close them again. What I was hoping for was that the glider would pick up enough speed to pull itself out of the death dive and fly out towards the valley. Praise be, it did, although it felt like the passing of an eon. Now I was relatively safe and I had chance to monitor the situation.

One thousand two hundred and fifty feet above the valley floor, moving in a straight and level direction instead of vertically, the crucial distinction between flying and falling. "Not too bad then" I thought. I later heard that most of the assembled crowd didn't bother approaching the edge as it was not expected to be a survivable situation. I am rather glad that they were wrong. The beginnings of the flight had brought back uncomfortable memories of another time when I was in an aircraft that did land vertically and I rejoiced that history was not about to repeat itself. Nevertheless I now considered myself to be safe, broadly speaking, and I got down to the task in hand, which was looking for thermals. As hard as I tried they were absent, so all I could do was chose a good landing area and make a decent attempt at getting down after the take off fiasco. Even this proved tricky as good landing areas, i.e. large flat uncluttered areas were worryingly absent. I ended up having to land on what appeared to be a vertical grass face. I impacted hard, rather like a fly landing on a wall. I remember thinking that I wasn't really impressing anyone today. After disentangling myself from the glider and ground, I looked back at the towering cliff to see how many had followed me. Unsurprisingly no one had. I realised that perhaps my take off was a little unconventional and my lack of success in finding thermals was also disappointing. As for the landing, well I can see that it could be viewed as unusual, so perhaps the lack of enthusiasm by the competition pilots could be understood to some degree or other. That said, from the comfort of the hillside I was expecting them to be made of sterner stuff. There was nothing for me to do now except lie down, sunbathe for a while and wait for the recovery car.

After about three hours, the car arrived to pick me up. Len was the driver and in the car we chatted about the flight:

"That was really impressive" he said with what I took as reverential tones.

Dunge Bottom

"Really?" I asked.

"Oh yea" he replied, "everyone else was so impressed they all packed up and went".

There was a strange mood hanging over the team as we made our way back to the hotel.

The next couple of days were weathered off and as our frustration reached boiling point we did start to get a bit impatient with our hotel twitters. We were saved from committing twitter genocide by the weather forecast on the third morning. It was going to be flyable again at last.

This time, because of the wind direction, we chose a site at Fairbourne. This was a six hundred feet high ridge overlooking Barmouth at the end of the river Barr estuary. The ridge extended to our right for about ten miles and finished at Cader Idris. It took about forty minutes to drive there and to our extreme pleasure there was a road almost at the top which meant only a small walk with our kit. We planned that some of us, me included, would leave our cars at the public car park at the bottom in case anyone landed out down there. We all carefully rigged our gliders. While we were doing this the wind changed direction and started blowing hard ninety degrees from our right, making it impossible to take off safely. The only thing for it was to lie down and wait for the wind to swing more onto the hill. Whilst waiting we were told that the task was to take off, turn right and fly along the valley right up to Cader Idris, carry on flying around the mountain into the valley behind and then fly onto a field at a cross roads just outside 'Machinelathe.' The first to land at the designated field would be the winner.

After a couple of hours we noticed that the wind was slowly coming more onto the slope, but still at too acute an angle to take off yet. There was a general wind flow funnelling down the Barmouth estuary towards the sea, but as the land heated up under the rising sun this flow started to be reversed and drew the wind in from the sea and on up the Barmouth estuary. Where the two air masses meet is called convergence. As the two opposing air masses collide the only way they can go is upwards and these are some of the best flying conditions if you can get in them. When we looked out to sea there was an enormous gathering of cumulus clouds showing the convergence line, which slowly, ever so slowly, started to move towards us and the land. We were convinced it could only be a matter of time until the wind arrived at the site and we would be able to fly. Over the next three hours the convergence line got nearer and nearer, but during this period the clouds had grown significantly in size, particularly in height, so much so that their appearance had the foreboding look of boiling black mayhem.

Eventually late in the afternoon the convergence arrived and I launched straight into the smooth powerful lift which accelerated me upwards towards the huge cloud line. The conditions were only too obviously excellent and there was a mad scramble for all the competition pilots to get into the air and start the task. I continued to climb with increasing acceleration, passing two thousand feet, three thousand feet and couldn't help notice that the lift was becoming stronger and stronger so much so it was when looking at my instruments I was now climbing at two thousand feet per minute, that's about twenty miles per hour, almost straight up. An amazing sensation but just a little bit scary. I looked around and saw the whole of the two teams were now in the same place as me, getting nearer and nearer to the line of the huge black clouds. Approaching five thousand feet and looking up I decided that I was now getting too close to the blackness and there was a very real risk of being sucked up into it. Being sucked up into the cloud would result in almost immediate disorientation, extreme turbulence and forces that could lead to the breakup of the glider and death. Interestingly enough, the rules stated that this manoeuvre was illegal. So as you plunged to certain death and contemplated your body being pulverised as you smashed into the mountainside, you also had the added irritation of knowing you were going to get points deducted. I did not fancy either so I needed to do something quickly to escape. I tried diving the glider downwards as fast as it would go and after a minute or two I saw that I was still going up at five hundred feet per minute. I wasn't the only one as looking around me I saw that all the pilots had realized the danger that we were all in and were trying to dive just as I was doing and failing. At least we would all get equal deductions, albeit posthumously. The clouds were getting closer and closer and all I could think of doing was to carry on diving at maximum speed whilst heading out to sea.

After what seemed a life time I eventually felt that the immense lift was decreasing and I was slowly gaining control of the situation as I flew out of the side of the convergence. I could start to breathe normally again. Mind you, being about five thousand feet up and five miles out to sea was nerve wrecking in itself. I can't swim and I couldn't fly back towards the land without hitting the convergence line again. I turned the glider slowly. Fortunately the line of convergence was slowly moving inland which meant I could gently follow it landwards and reach sanctuary. I was beginning to feel in control again as I arrived over Barmouth at about two thousand feet, which, if you have ever been to Barmouth you will know, is arguably the best way to see it.

John Clarke

The competition pilots had dissipated now and were out of sight, so I just started milling around and enjoying the flying in the incredibly smooth air. On glancing down I just happened to notice that a blue and silver Ford Granada was driving out of the car park and disappearing up the valley towards Cader Idris. Nice looking car I thought, very similar to mine, followed by.

"What the hell?! It's my Granada." Some bastard had nicked it. I spiralled down as fast as possible to lose height and try and get my car back. Landing right next to the car park, I ran over and confirmed that it was indeed my car that had been stolen. Looking around I saw one of our team loading his car nearby.

"Some bastards nicked my Granada" I blurted out.

"No they haven't" was his calm reply.

"Yes they bloody have, I've just seen it driving away" I shouted back.

"It's OK, Len has borrowed it to go and retrieve some of our team who have landed out just down the valley" he smiled back.

"Oh for God's sake" was all I could muster in relief.

Eventually it came to the penultimate evening of the competition and the scores were level pegging. I feel that I must mention at this point that the time we spent flying against the Frenchies taught me a lot about their psychological makeup. You see they cheated. They were blatantly caught flying at nine thirty in the evening when they all should have landed at six thirty, like all the Brits did. One of tasks was to fly as far as possible from take off and the furthest would be the winner. The only condition was that all pilots should have landed and telephoned the competition control by six thirty pm. So obviously the longer one flew the further the potential distance flown would be. The French denied it, of course, but the evidence was irrefutable, we even had it recorded on film. Their protestations were many and varied, including "it wasn't me, it was filmed on another day, go on then prove it was me", all in atrocious French accents. Complete bollocks of course. The French Team Captain had the audacity to hitch a lift back at nine forty five in the evening. He even asked one of the competition marshals for the lift. So there we are, we had them bang to rights.

We, the Brits thought that this was great, as they would be disqualified for the day's task and it would not matter if we lost on the last day, as we couldn't then be beaten. There was great rejoicing at Team Britain Hotel, but we were naïve and had yet to learn how formidable our French opposition really were. Their cunning plan was simple in its audacity. They went to the adjudicating committee and told them that if they were disqualified they would pack up and go home.

There was then long involved negotiations between the committee and the French Team manager which went along the lines of,

"This an international competition, you can't just leave can you?"

"Oui"

But what about the press conference, you've got to be there,."

"Non"

But what about the civic reception, the mayor and the sponsors will expect to see you all there"

Sound of 'Gallic shrug'

A light slowly illuminated the minds of the competition committee showing that they would not win these negotiations. They were dealing with a race who think nothing of sinking a Green Peace ship at berth in a harbour and burning sheep on the dockside as a protest. A hang gliding competition committee was "petit problemé". Outside the committee room we were joyous at the proceedings although we were not actually privy to them as the hearing was behind closed doors. However our mood was very upbeat. We thought we had won. Unknown to us the competition committee, realizing that they were in a no win situation, capitulated and reinstated the points to the French team.

"Bastards", we all thought and definitely said to anyone who would listen.

Our twitters were very interested in the day's proceedings and try as hard as they could; they had extreme difficulty in comprehending the technicalities of the French Teams cheating tactics. After all how could anyone take advantage of their nice young men? Continuing, they told us, even the young French people must have some niceness about them, although some of our twitters started to mutter gain about the Vichy French antics in the war. We did notice that it took very little encouragement for them to start muttering about the war and the "goings on"! We were shocked and disappointed but we pulled ourselves together and hatched a plan for the final day. We called it, Plan STBF. Screw The Bloody French!

The final day dawned bright, clouded over, then brightened again. The mood in our hotel was sombre and very determined. There was much talk of Agincourt and other such times. The plan was set. We drove to the top of Constitution Hill, which overlooks the town.

The final task of the competition was to take off from Constitution Hill, fly along the front of the hotels on the seafront of Aberystwyth, cross the estuary, onto the cliffs beyond, and then to the beach at Newquay, some nineteen miles away. The fastest would win. Simple. The Frenchies were not used to flying when there was any wind and today on the cliffs of the hill it was blowing between twenty five and thirty miles per hour. We had chosen the location with care and to our delight they were looking worried. Len called us altogether to discuss tactics. His idea was deceptively simple, and turning to me he issued the following orders. "Clarkey I want you launch first but make the take off look really scary, even scream a bit and when you fly over the estuary make it look as if you aren't going to make it and have to land in the sea. Hopefully we'll psych them out and they won't want to play anymore." Len had another small flourish to his plan. A local Welsh pilot would loudly pronounce that no one had ever made it across the estuary yet! A brilliant wind up! I thought it sounded simple, I mean, if anyone could fake a dodgy flight I, with my voluminous experience, was perfect. In, what was for me, a relatively relaxed frame of mind, I kitted up, made my checks and approached the cliff edge. This was harder than I expected as I was buffeted around by the increasingly strong wind, so much so that some of my compatriots dashed forward to help me steady the wings of the glider. At last I got to the cliff edge and looking round I saw smug grins from the Brits and concern on the faces of the enemy.

"Impossible, merde, il est fou", were comments that caught my ears. The plan seems to be working already.

"Well here goes", I thought and made a promise to myself to make it look scary. The wind was about thirty plus miles per hour now, and quite gusty. I launched myself off the cliff into the boisterous air. It was really rough and I was being pitched downwards and sideways directly towards the cliff edge.

"Bloody Hell!".

John Clarke

The situation was deteriorating rapidly. I hoped that the Frenchies could see the look in my eyes, as I careered towards them. It was a pretty convincing display of 'scary' that did not test my acting skills in any way. It was the look of a pilot who decided that he was now not in control of the situation and that adrenaline was brown and living somewhere within the dark recesses of his flying suit. Fortunately the glider managed to sort things out and I made off towards the seafront at Aberystwyth, soaring above the roofs of the hotels. The air had now smoothed out and I was feeling a little more comfortable.

It was time to cross the estuary. I looked across the gap between the hotels and the far cliffs. I couldn't help but notice that it seemed quite a big gap, a bloody big gap, in fact with lots of water underneath it. Getting back towards the take off was impossible so I had no choice but to aim for the cliffs on the other side. I knew that the tale told by the local pilot was a wind up so I was quite confidant as I headed out across the water. After a few minutes of peaceful flying I looked across to the far cliffs. To my chagrin I noticed that I was no longer looking down on the cliffs but looking up at them instead. I wondered if Len would now be satisfied that the scary bit of the plan had been achieved, as I started to become a little scared myself. The glider descended further and I started to do a pretty good impression of someone who was faced with a long swim, or a short drown. I really hoped the French were taking all this in. My feet started bicycling desperately. Perhaps, I could walk on water? I thought about praying, but I couldn't remember who the patron saint of idiots was. Whoever it is he must have been listening. With my feet almost trailing in the sea, I slid onto the very bottom part of the cliffs, and the glider now stopped descending and began imperceptibly at first to climb in the rising air in front of the cliffs. That was my salvation and gave me the chance to make the finishing line.

After the last ten minutes the rest of the trip down the cliffs to Newquay was an anti climax and even when I dropped low enough to skim the roofs of a line of beach huts, to a jump a gap in the cliffs, it didn't even cause me to break sweat. Forty five minutes later I made it to the landing field on the cliff edge just behind a line of trees at Newquay village. As I approached the

field I became concerned because it was right on the cliff edge and you had to approach it from behind trees, which you first needed to clear, to land in the field. It all looked very suspicious and I was concerned that I would be encountering some rotor. I had never flown in rotor before and this landing field looked the perfect breeding ground for this phenomenon. Rotor is when air behind obstacles becomes disturbed and is random in nature, certainly not smooth, it shows itself by changes in wind direction sometimes as much as one hundred and eighty degrees with huge changes in speed as well. Handled badly, it can somewhat spoil your day. I gave a sigh of resignation. Our wonderful competition organisers had chosen the final landing field on a cliff edge and having a line of tall trees on its downward edge! It won't surprise you to hear, therefore, that I got sunk out just behind the trees, just managing to climb over the tops of them, kicking the topmost branches in an effort to get clear before landing, in pieces, facing the way I had just come. Dramatic or what? Especially to the assembled gathering of competition marshalls and judges. Also really quite scary, after all I had battled with the take off on the cliff edge, only just made it across the estuary, played with the roofs of the beach huts, not to crash and burn in the final landing field. No problem however I was still alive.

Over the next couple of hours I had the privilege of watching a steady succession of British pilots arriving in the landing field, albeit pointing in varied directions as they did so and with varying pieces of broken glider about them. In fact one of them on approaching the tall trees didn't make it over them but impaled himself on a branch. It soon became apparent that we had won as almost no French pilots actually arrived. My theatricals in the early part of the task had genuinely scared off almost all the French team who had decided the task was too dangerous.

I travelled back to our hotel with Len and we had great fun reliving the day especially how well the 'wind up' went. Len was very proud of his ploy and I was extremely cheerful about my part in it.

"I'm bloody glad that local pilot was winding us up about crossing the estuary, eh Len" I chatted jovially.

"What do you mean?" he said with a puzzled expression,

"Well I didn't think I was going to make it, but knowing it was wind up kept me going"

"Clarkey" he said, "take a deep breath and try and stay calm, m'boy, no one has ever got across it. You were the first"

St Jude was his name, the patron saint of desperate causes. I think he was in Aberystwyth that day.

It was with great rejoicing that we made it back to our hotel. We were loud and hearty and woke some of the twitters up. They greeted us with their usual chorus.

"Did you have a nice day dears?" We answered in the affirmative and were somewhat surprised to discover that perhaps they had been listening more carefully than we had previously given them credit for, when they asked their supplementary question.

"Did we beat the bastards?"

14

Thermals

I have suddenly realised that I have been referring to thermals quite extensively throughout and you might, dear reader, have some lack of understanding about them. So I thought I would make a small detour to put your mind at rest.

Well obviously I am not referring to ones undergarments, although having said that I have been known to wear them twice to preserve some vestige of body heat whilst flying in the chill winter winds. I only wore them twice since co-incidentally I ended up in A&E Depts., on the two occasions, enjoying some form of traumatic injury. I cannot tell you how embarrassing it is the be in said A&E Dept., having one's outer layers of clothing removed by the hardnosed nursing staff to reveal the creamy off white full body thermal underwear complete with cat flap. No, the thermals I am referring to are bubbles or columns of relatively warm air that gliders can rise in up to quite dizzy

Dunge Bottom

heights. I just thought that you might be interested to hear a bit about them especially as they are an intrinsic part of gliding. It is they that have made the enormous cross country distances possible.

Well here's how they work......

The sun comes up, heats up the ground, which in turn begins to heat up the air that is sitting over the ground. After a while, the bubble of air gets hotter and bigger until it reaches a state where it is so buoyant that it breaks from the ground due to the fact that warm air is lighter than cold air or it is disturbed by say a cow walking into it and pushing it away from the surface. Now this bubble can be the size of a small balloon or the size of Greater Manchester. The former would be difficult for a glider to use due to its small size but the latter would be brilliant for the opposite reason. The speed that these thermals can go up is anything from just a few feet per minute to several thousand feet per minute. However the latter can be a bit scary as say a thermal climbing at two thousand feet per minute equates to about twenty miles per hour. upwards. The thermal will continue to rise whilst it is warmer than the surrounding air, but as you will all remember from Mr. Playll's physics lessons at school when he told us, as air goes up so it cools down, due to the heat being given up to the surrounding atmostphere. So whilst the glider is in the thermal and going up nicely, it is only a transient thing since once the bottom of the bubble leaves the ground, then it is the beginning of the end. Consequently a thermal has an average life in this world of about twenty minutes.

It is a fantastic feeling gently going around in circles and climbing higher and ever higher as the earth disappears beneath you and all the hills and bumps seemingly appear to flatten out. Unfortunately of course there is always a payback time, what goes up must come down. Although you have bits of warm air going up you also have bits of cold air coming down, which can bring you back down on the ground very quickly indeed...Bugger. To give an illustration of the power of thermals I ask that you read on.

A Thunder Storm and an Alp.

The competition pilots were assembled high up near the top edge of the tree line on the almost sheer mountain side overlooking an immensely deep Austrian alpine valley. They came from all over the world to attend this hang gliding competition and some were somewhat disturbed to see that their launch site was actually a specially built wooden ramp, about 6 feet wide and 10 feet long which jutted out over the tall pine trees that continued all the way down the 6000 feet to the valley floor. It was a baking hot day, with a cold northerly wind blowing which meant that there was a very big temperature difference between the heat of the sun warming the ground and the cold air. This had the effect of making the thermals very strong and powerful indeed. As a result there were large numbers of towering boiling white cumulus clouds, which progressively grew bigger and bigger and blacker and blacker as the day went on, with some eventually developing into the evil power of thunderstorms. Luckily enough for these pilots it seemed that the worst of the thunder storm activity was holding in the adjacent valley to that the competition was being held in.

Throughout the day there was a steady succession of pilots conquering the unnerving tiny wooden take off ramp, before hurling themselves off it and skimming over the trees below, which seemed to be reaching up trying to ensnare

Dunge Bottom

them in theirclutches. The task for the pilots was to fly over landmarks on the valley floor, take a photograph to prove that the landmark had actually been reached then land as near to the bull's eye target on the ground, all in the fastest possible time. As the afternoon wore on it was noticed by all left on the mountain side that a particularly venomous thunderstorm was now quickly building in the adjacent valley. It towered high into the sky, with thunder and lightning shaking and illuminating the very earth with their intensity. Many of the remaining pilots cast anxious glances across to the neighbouring valley but it seemed that the monster was trapped there and showed no immediate sign of hopping over the dividing mountains into their competition area. The competition marshals however were very uneasy with the close proximity of this particular thunderstorm and closed the task. This meant that no one had to fly and most of the pilots decided that this was where discretion was better than valour and de rigged their gliders before returning back to the valley floor the same way that they had arrived at the mountain top, by cable car.

For reasons we will never know three pilots chose not to follow the others lead but to fly straight down to the lush green landing fields far below. Shortly after the last one had launched from the lofty perch flying out into the thin Alpine air the black boiling behemoth finally stepped over the dividing range and into the path of the flyers. With breath taking speed and seemingly from nowhere the sky became black as night, lit only by the searing flashes of the lightning. Savage swirling winds ripped along the earth like dervishes, all of this now reaching out towards the three remaining flyers. They had managed to descend nearly all of the 6000 feet from take off and so now could almost taste the safety of the valley floor. All three were now low enough to the landing area to drop their legs out of their harnesses in final preparation for landing and safety. They were all between fifty and one hundred feet from salvation. But the monster had other ideas.

Dear reader, I wonder if for one moment you can you just try and put yourself in their position? You are almost able to reach down and touch the ground, you can smell the scent of the lush flowers bedecking the alpine meadow just beneath your feet, but there is a vicious gusty wind hitting you with unbelievable force from all directions seemingly at the same time. You are being lifted up and smashed down again with ferocious savagery, the glider is being turned through 360 degrees and you realize that you no longer have any control of it. You are under the shadow of this beast which is now reaching down and touching your sanctuary that is the ground. Then it starts to rain. Not just rain but rain falling with such intensity that it hits you as hard as needles.

You have no protection from this unending beating.

You now realise that instead of getting nearer the ground you are actually climbing into the great black maw of the storm. The blackness engulfs you. You have no idea what is happening all you can sense is the apocalyptic violence which relentlessly smashes you around. Within seconds you are now completely disorientated, completely at the mercy of this storm. Blinded by the flashes of lightning all around you, how can they not fry you alive, such is their proximity. Your nose is filled with the pungent smell of ozone released by the lightning. Surely your ears must be bleeding now as the deafening claps of thunder resonate throughout your body. All your senses are being mercilessly and overwhelmingly savaged. In a briefest moment of relative calm, you glance at your altimeter, it shows twelve thousand

Dunge Bottom

feet. Your very own Armageddon begins all over again, how much higher can the storm take you. It is at this moment that your glider can no longer stand the enormous forces hitting it and you both feel and hear the aluminium tubes of the airframe snapping under their tortuous loads. Your glider is no longer a flying machine just a dis-jointed assembly of aluminium,sail material and you. But no one can hear you scream.

Some days later Mountain Rescue Teams found two pilots high up on the mountain side with both their gliders and themselves smashed beyond recognition.

The third, in a final act of desperation and being unable to dive his glider down fast enough to reach the ground, deployed his emergency reserve parachute. He was hoovered up into the writhing mass of that black world now completely filling the valley. His body was later found twenty five miles away having obviously been subjected to tremendous forces and at frightening altitudes dying of oxygen starvation and freezing temperatures.

You might think this is an isolated incident but something a little similar did happen at Hay Bluff near Hay on Wye. This is a fabulous and famous flying site which is about eight hundred feet high having one side about fifteen miles long whilst the other, approximately two miles long, overlooks the plains of Mid Wales. Much excellent flying has been done here over the years and it attracts flyers from all over the country. Its downside is that there is no road near the top and the walk up whilst initially looking innocuous, is a real killer. In fact it is so bad a walk pilots are sometimes tempted to fly off the top even if conditions are not necessarily entirely suitable or completely safe rather than face the walk back down again.

Such was the case when an English pilot considered

John Clarke

taking off under a completely overcast sky one April day.

The cloud base was only a few hundred feet above the top of the hill and the wind at take off seemed quite variable and gusty. Shortly after take off he found himself in rising air which he started to explore by turning in it. Suddenly the rising air became far stronger and he rapidly approached cloud base. He tried everything he could to lose height and stay below the enveloping cloud, but to no avail and he was drawn up into it. He simply did not realize that it was a thunderstorm which was embedded within the overall cloud sheet and consequently hidden from view, as at that time the thunder and lightning had not started.

He was more fortunate than those Austrian flyers for he was eventually forcibly ejected out of the side of the thunder head having been trashed around inside it for forty five minutes, completely out of sight of the ground and reaching heights of fifteen thousand feet.

15

A Bridge, A Prostitute and Innsbruck

I can't actually remember if I did mention to Jane and Malcolm that we needed to cross the Austrian border, ideally in the early hours of the morning and at some desolate outpost somewhere in the mountains? Jane and Malcolm are long standing dear friends who we met when they came on a hang gliding course. Jane is a lovely, giggly, bubbly young chum with an ever ready smile. Malcolm is the quietly spoken killer type with a gentle smile and who is normally to be found lurking at the back of the class planning all sorts of mischief. We had to try and keep everything low key you see. I also probably forgot to mention that the four hang gliders on the roof of the car might not actually have all the necessary paperwork required to get them into Austria. These minor details are very easy to overlook when planning a skiing and flying holiday after all.

We all thought it a good idea to go on a skiing/flying holiday to Austria and to save money we travelled by car.

Dunge Bottom

This was particularly important as we had a small Did to take with us. Did was our first born daughter who was only about twelve months old and was very much looking forward to her first skiing holiday, at least she showed what I interpreted as enthusiasm. Well, she made gurgling noises every time I showed the ski brochure.

I realise that Did might be considered a strange name for a young baby, but it all stemmed from when she started to make her first noises which sounded very much, like

"DiddDiddDiddDidd...........hence Did or Diddy. Mind you if you think that is strange our second production, another girl, has been called Potts n Pans, Potts, N'Hausen, Pustule and Orifice. The latter two she very much enjoyed until she attended middle school and actually learnt what these affectionate terms meant. I must admit there was a bit of tension between father and daughter for a little while after that. Anyway she's now called Potts which seems acceptable to all concerned.

Back to the story...

We set off from Jane and Malcolm's house, near St. Albans, in our little red diesel Peugeot 205, with four adults, Did in her baby seat in the middle of the back seats, a trailer hanging off the back for all our luggage and four hang gliders on the roof. Because the hang gliders were about twenty two feet long and the car was only twelve feet long it did mean that there was an enormous overhang at the front, which basically gave the appearance of travelling at night and in permanent darkness. This resulted having to drive with the headlights on all the time. We soon got used to it, however.

The journey to Austria went very well despite the cramped conditions and our Did was marvellous, only getting grumpy every fifteen minutes. However the

John Clarke

Memsahib and Jane who sat either side of Did developed a foolproof way of keeping the child amused and quiet. For without warning and at the top of their voices they would roar out;

"Day Oh, De-ee-O, Daylight Come and me Wanna Go home".

This greatly amused Did, but proved to be a little trying to the occupants of the front seats. Luckily, this only went on for...twelve hundred miles.

As I said, the plan was to enter Austria under the cover of darkness via an obscure customs post high up in the Alps and then wend our way down to Innsbruck to meet up with our contacts, and offload "the goods". We arrived a little later than planned and entered the centre of Innsbruck at three in the morning. There was a chill in the air and the city's lights shone harshly through the mist rising up from the river. We had driven into a John Le Carre novel. Now this was long before the invention of mobile phones - yes, yes there was such a time. We had lost the directions to the rendezvous point and now were hopelessly lost, however I did have a telephone number to call. This was still tricky because we had no Austrian schillings only Austrian paper money which the telephone boxes obviously wouldn't accept.

Now I had read John le Carre so I considered myself quite the sophisticate when it came to surviving in a European City. I spied a scantily dressed young lady walking across a bridge spanning the River Inn. A marvellous opportunity, I seized it. I must point out at this time my only German was to be able to ask for a piece of Black Forest Gateau with cream or the phrase "I am coming for you Karla". So trying to ask for change for the telephone call was far beyond my ability.

Dunge Bottom

I stopped the car which, by now, had the windows steamed up a little, somewhat obscuring the occupants. Leaning out through the drivers window I waved an Austrian ten schilling note and called out to the scantily clad young lady. In my best sign language I tried to explain that I needed some change for the note in my hand to make a telephone call. I confess that my macaroon signing was a failure; I can put it no less strongly that. The young lady glanced across, smiled oddly as I thought at the time and began to approach with a purpose and intent which I found a little unnerving. Even more unnerving at this moment was the sight of a police car slowly turning onto the bridge and approaching us also with a purpose and intent or so it seemed. "Jolly good", I thought, I can ask both of them for change or even perhaps directions, what a relief. My hopes were dimmed a little Malcolm saying something like..........

"Oh Shit, now we're for it. You bloody imbecile what on earth are you playing at?"

At this moment there was a united cry from all adult members of the group, except me, of course requesting that I just drive off now, straight away with no arguments and get the hell out of here before the police and the scantily clad young lady get any closer. I started to query what they meant exactly when at this point Malcolm quite firmly and seemingly in no mood to be argued with muttered.

"Bloody drive...now!!"

I drove.

The gang were very kind to me later, pointing out how my innocent efforts to change a note of the Austrian realm for coins for the phone box could easily be misinterpreted by both the prostitute and the police officers. It could have been worse, the Polezei could have heard me shout the 'Karla' phrase.

John Clarke

And So To War

It was about eight o' clock on a bleak cold November night. There was mayhem in our old kitchen, I had just trodden on the cat, accidentally of course, but the children were accusing me of attempted pussycide, the cat seemed to agree and was wailing and spitting at me; I needed sanctuary and quickly.

Luckily it arrived by way of a telephone call.

"Hi John here" I announced into the ether, fully expecting to be asked if I was the person responsible for paying the telephone bill, you know the scene I'm sure. In actual fact, there was a pause followed by; in hushed tones....

"Is that John"

"Yes"

"John Clarke"

"Could be... "I was beginning to get annoyed and a little suspicious now and didn't want to give too much away. It could be a kitchen/conservatory/double glazing sales person after all.

"It's Phil" the voice said.

I quickly went through the eighty three Phils that I knew. I still could not place the voice.

"Phil who?", I couldn't stand the suspense any longer.

"Phil P, are you alone?"

Now I knew who Phil P was and so immediately went into a gentle rant and pointing out that I wasn't actually alone at this particular moment due to the family, the cat ....

"Enough, stop it" I noticed an air of exasperation in his voice.

"Listen very carefully, and do exactly as I say. Pack two suitcases, don't forget your passport. A car will collect you

Dunge Bottom

on Wednesday evening at seven to take you to Brize Norton. Be ready and say nothing to anyone. Should the family ask you are going on a business trip for a couple of months. You won't be able to speak to them whilst you are away. Goodbye."

"Bloody Hell, shit " I muttered. It was actually going to happen. I never thought it would happen in my wildest dreams and I can tell you I frequently have some of those!

You see, it all started in spring when I was approached by an inventor I shall call Phil P., who wanted my help to test a special sort of microlight. Phil was an RAF Officer who worked in a "special section" which he couldn't really discuss with me. He wasn't your typical RAF officer, you would expect to see a tall, broad shouldered, narrow waisted flying type with a moustache that looked like it had its own hairdressers, talking loudly to all and sundry in incomprehensible flying banter. In fact Phil was a very amiable slightly rotund sort of guy who had an infectious enthusiasm for life generally and aviation particularly.

"Fancy helping me out with an idea" he asked nonchalantly one summer day when, yet again, we were waiting for the flying conditions to improve.

"Sure Phil, what's going on?" was my immediate reply. I was always interested in new things and was keen to find out what Phil was after.

"I need someone who can fly microlights to test a bit of an invention of mine"

You would think, after my previous test flight experiences, I would know better. Well, I didn't and I agreed to meet up with him at RAF Cranwell one June afternoon.

Now RAF Cranwell has a bit of a history. From 1915 it has been the primary training base for RAF officers and the air

John Clarke

force's finest have all, at some point, walked its hallowed ground. One of the pupils was Sir Frank Whittle and it was on this base that the first flight of the Gloster E28/39 jet plane took place. As a child I remember being struck by the iconic images of that snub nose craft lifting into the air. Its pilot was Flight Lieutenant Philip 'Gerry' Sayer. Just over a year after testing the jet engine Sayers flew from RAF Acklington to try out a gun sight in a Hawker Typhoon. He never returned. I hoped I wasn't about to share his fate.

Phil met me at the gate and took me straight away to see the prototype. It was a microlight, but one which could fold down very small and be easily assembled and had a set of wheels on it so you could take off by running or using the wheels which you could later land on. The framing was black painted aluminium with an all black sail. The pilot would lie down in the harness just inches off the floor and take off and land in this position.

"What do you think?" asked Phil

"Well it's a very attractive shade of black" I said, trying to be helpful and trying to figure out what the unique selling point of the black contraption would be. I was imagining Phil was going to launch this new idea on the unsuspecting microlight world.

"It's got to be black" he said.

Phil wanted me to have a fly round in the black beast, and of course I leapt at the opportunity. I struggled into the harness with a bit of difficulty especially as there was a small two stroke engine tucked inside it with a two bladed wooden propeller sticking out at the back. Phil helped me check I was clipped in properly and showed me how to use the throttle, which was a lever fitted to the control bar of the glider. His briefing was simple (memories flooded back),

201

Dunge Bottom

"Take off requires full power, wait for the aircraft to lift off which it will do on its own, enjoy the handling and, when ready, land, but stay prone and use the wheels"

As Phil had described, the aircraft took off on its own after about seventy five yards of being bounced around on the rough grass strip. It climbed gently at about three hundred feet per minute which I thought was an impressive rate. I flew around for about half an hour gently exploring its handling and performance. It really was easy to fly and good fun Mind you the landing felt very odd staying in the prone position with your face and gentleman parts so near the ground!

Phil asked if I thought this idea would work? This confused me a little because I had no idea what he was talking about. In the end I had to ask him just to tell me in simple terms (I am that sort of person after all) what was going on.

He then made a startling statement.........

"You must tell no one about this and if you agree to help the scheme you will have to sign the Official Secrets Act".

"Good grief " I thought.

"You see" he continued, "in the very near future we are going to war in the Middle East. We are expecting losses from our Tornado squadrons and I have been tasked to come up with an effective aircrew retrieval system.

He explained that the plan is to load one of these machines into a spare fuel pod on a Tornado which will go out to the site of a downed aircraft and drop the pod off by parachute and at night.

"The crew will assemble it, and fly under cover of darkness back towards friendly forces, utilising night vision goggles. Your job is to come out with me and train the Tornado aircrews on how to use and fly it."

"Hells Bells, I'm a lover not a fighter" I thought.

I then thought about it a little more, and came to the conclusion that, "Bloody Hell" would be a much more appropriate response. In fact it was so appropriate I repeated it several times.

Returning to the night of the phone call, I am very glad to say that a day later I received another call from Phil P., standing me down from the operation as the RAF were going to use the American Search and Rescue helicopters initially and Phil's idea would be kept in reserve just in case. I was both relieved and disappointed at this stand down call. It would have been great to go out and do one's bit to help in the war. Of course I would never have been able to talk about it not even to my loved ones.

As it turned out the expected attrition rate for the RAF was very low and they easily managed with the normal rescue missions by the RAF and American search and rescue helicopter squadrons.

The End Or Is It?

Well dear reader you made it, battered and bruised I expect, but hopefully still alive and with some semblance of sanity left intact.

You may even be wondering about the title of the book, Dunge Bottom, and I wouldn't blame you if you were. You see it does exist hidden deep within a Derbyshire Dale. It captured my imagination when I first clapped my rheumy eyes upon it to such an extent that I adopted a   second alter ego, now not just Clarke of Adventure but also Dunge Bottom.

So me and my alter egos, Clarke of Adventure and Dunge Bottom are about to sally forth yet again to perhaps bring you further tales of the unexpected in another offering, calling on the people and incidents that were enjoyed in my years attempting to teach mere mortals to fly various forms of flying machines. So until we meet again across the written page let your mind run free and be not afraid to go through any door that opens before you.

Enjoy your adventures.

Acknowledgments

Where to start dear reader, where to start? Well actually that isn't too difficult a problem. You see my parents, Fred and Mumsie, unhesitatingly encouraged me to give up a safe but boring day job and start my own hang gliding business; so one can clearly lay the blame at their door.

PJ the Memsahib, for putting up with me and the strangely uncertain world of micro aviation for so long and for my girls, Didd and Potts who were never ever allowed to speak whilst the weather forecast was on the TV. Without the support of all the above I would never have collected such a plethora of adventures and experiences over something like the quarter of a century that this book spans.

Additionally, this book would never have seen the light of day at all without the laughs, encouragement and downright bullying of my publisher, Matt Webb, who against almost impossible odds led me kicking and screaming into the real world of writing. He gave me the hope that people might actually enjoy reading it and even possibly laugh at some of the antics. His faith and belief kept me going, along with strong black coffee of course.

What you have here is the combination of contributions from all named, I am merely the scribe.

Lightning Source UK Ltd.
Milton Keynes UK
UKOW011004081011

179978UK00001B/6/P

9 780956 844705